CONIFA:

Football for the Forgotten

CONIFA:
Football for the Forgotten

By James Hendicott

First Printing: 2019

ISBN   978-0-244-17363-0

www.hendicottwriting.com

Ordering Information: via the above website, or email jameshendicott.jh@gmail.com

Special discounts are available on quantity purchases by corporations, associations, educators, and others. For details, contact the author.

Dedicated to my wife Helena and son Adam for their love, and tolerance of my quirky passions.

When I first met Helena as an emigrant in Seoul back in 2007, I was going through a period of extreme frustration with football, and when she asked if I was interested in sport, I told her I wasn't. It felt true at the time, and I suspect it was an answer she quite liked. A few months later, we watched the Birmingham derby in a boisterous pub in the early hours of a Monday morning. I'm an Aston Villa fan, and the K-league had slowly reignited my love of the game. On that particular day, my team swept aside the other half of the city, I got on the pints in celebration, and that particular illusion of disinterest was shattered forever.

Twelve years later, as I dedicate myself to projects like this, Adam has become my little assistant on the terraces of Dublin non-league clubs, and Helena's become the kind of incredible life partner who hears ideas like 'I'd like to write a book about international football teams that only kind of unofficially exist' and actually suggests I give it a go.

You're both wonderful, I love you, and I thank you for making this book possible. And I'm sorry, Helena, it turns out I am interested!

Introduction

"How can you tell a 15-year-old boy he can't play top-level football, because of politics?" asks Bülent Aytaç, manager of the Northern Cyprus football team. "We would like to play with FIFA. We're an island. Half of an island. So football for us is a very small pond. These players are sharks in that pond. We have to be allowed to play. FIFA won't have us, so this is how we compete."

CONIFA is the footballing answer to a host of questions most people are lucky enough to never have to ask. Questions like what happens to a country's football team when the international community rejects them? What if, for social, political or historical reasons, the idea of playing for the country whose borders constrain you is beyond the pale? What if your people are Tibetans, or Tamils, and no longer have a land to call their own?

The minnows of FIFA's international game obtain a certain notoriety. Every European football fan has something to say on San Marino, Liechtenstein and Gibraltar, for example, ranging from mild amusement to a love of the underdog. There are occasional calls for tiered qualifying in big competitions, but few question these sides' right to exist. But what about Monaco? What about Tuvalu? What about Vatican City, or the Isle of Man? What if you're a member of a group that tends to exist, at best, on the fringes of the sporting arena: a Roma gypsy, or a stateless refugee?

CONIFA - the Confederation of Independent Football Associations - aims to fill those gaps, giving representation to minority groups, unrecognised nations and other entities. Though you'll rarely hear of the teams involved, CONIFA say their sides currently represent a total of more than 330 million people, close to 5% of the world's population.

This book is about what happened when CONIFA's teams came together to play in their third World Football Cup, in London in 2018. It is also - perhaps more importantly - about the journeys taken

1

to get there. It's about the protests and the controversies, the financial constraints, the drop-outs, the politics, and the passion of the fans. It celebrates teams who came to win, and others who won their own victories simply by turning up.

Of course, it's also about what happened on the pitch. We'll be going game by game in London, all 48 of them. That includes exploring the unknown players playing outside their own regions for the first time, and former World Cup stars and Champions League-level stand-outs turning out for the sides they feel best represent them. We'll drop in on all the action: the goals, the passion, and the glory.

The organisation is not without its critics. In fact, there are plenty of them. We'll take a glance at why some believe CONIFA is a Russian-backed political influencer, and why several national governments tried to intervene to prevent the London tournament taking place at all. Then there's the mid-tournament withdrawal of founder member Ellan Vannin from the London event, and its knock-on effects, plus the money issues that have plagued the organisation throughout their existence.

CONIFA, at its heart, is an organisation for the unrepresented. Their approximately 50 (and growing) teams - from Tibet to Greenland, Darfur to Tuvalu - are rejected by the footballing world. They play anyway, often overcoming unimaginably challenging obstacles to do so, sometimes at substantial personal risk. There are arrests, bankruptcies, bitter allegations, and high-level political pressures, yet the show goes on. This is CONIFA's story.

Matchday 1: Jetlag and Dancing...

It's mid-afternoon on an ordinary Thursday in early summer when I roll into Gander Green Lane, home of Surrey non-league side Sutton United. As I stroll through the tumble-down turnstiles, a team of scrawny, energetic East Africans emerge from their team bus, singing. They chant, holler and dance their way through the club doors. Their black and orange tracksuits bob and weave to the harmonies they create. 'We Will Conquer', they harmonise, as they snake through the 80s-style clubhouse, and on into their changing room.

A few minutes later, the same men emerge from the bowels of Gander Green, nervously stepping through the caged tunnel and out onto the pitch. Mentor (and former Liverpool and Zimbabwe international goalkeeper) Bruce Grobbelaar and manager Justin Walley trail in their wake.

Dressed in their vibrant team colours, black shirts with swirling Ndebele patterns across the chest, several players reach down to pick at the artificial pitch, running their hands through its blades and bouncing the glistening tournament football against its perfectly even, faux-grass surface. They look at each other and chuckle, glance at the gathering crowd, then set about testing the run of the ball.

This team are Matabeleland. They represent a minority group from a backwater region of southern and western Zimbabwe, and have spent months training on dry, trash-strewn and often grassless pitches to be here. Most of the team are abroad for the first time. They've never come across 3G - the high-end fake grass that's common at English lower-tier grounds - until right before they have to play on it.

The Matabeleland region's history is dark. After Zimbabwe won independence in the early 80s, tensions between the local Ndebele people (for whom the region is named) and new ruler Robert Mugabe and his Shona people spilled over. The most vicious attack came through the appalling Gukurahundi massacres.

Gukurahundi translates as "the early rain which washes away the chaff before the spring rains," a shocking euphemism for massacres that saw an estimated 20,000 Ndebele civilians summarily executed by the North Korean-trained 5th Brigade of the Zimbabwean army. As well as the deaths, many more from the area were sent for brainwashing in "re-education camps". Mugabe's army also restricted food supplies to the area, causing many Ndebele to starve.

There have been efforts in Matabeleland to have the perpetrators of the 80s attacks tried for war crimes at The Hague. A separatist Matabeleland Freedom Party was established in exile in South Africa as recently as 2006, and recent events after Mugabe resigned the nation's leadership have again led to tribal tensions. The nation's old wounds, clearly, are far from healing.

Whether Matabeleland is a nation, though, remains up for debate, regardless of the existence of the government in exile. The team's visas only cleared a few days before travel to London, and not without issues, but they're here, and all set to play. Their opening opponents in Group C, Padania, from the north of Italy, are widely considered one of the strongest teams at the CONIFA's tournament. This is not international football as we know it.

There are around 300 diehard football enthusiasts, a spattering of CONIFA volunteers and a few curious journalists in Gander Green, a place long known for its FA Cup upsets. Nobody knows much about any of the players. Instead of the rigorous press process that's become standard in international football, to collect my media pass, I simply have to give my first name to someone in a CONIFA shirt. In exchange, I take an anonymous, plastic-covered business card, that short interaction sufficient to clear me to attend any of 48 tournament games across the coming nine days.

Hosts Sutton United, currently playing at English conference level, just missed out on the FA Cup quarter finals here in 2017. They were unfortunate to be beaten 2-0 by Arsenal, having already seen off Leeds United and AFC Wimbledon. They also famously defeated then top-tier Coventry City at Gander Green in 1989.

The ground has a feel of a run-down social hub, a spot that evokes English football in decades past, far from the plush world of corporate boxes and three-figure ticket options. There's one short stand of seats, several with hand-penned, sticky-taped name labels indicating their regular-season occupants, and covered terraces on the other three sides. The corner standing areas have barriers of flaky yellow paint, and the back of the terraces feature stickers proclaiming the glory of non-league football and pie and chips, and poking fun at Prime Minister Theresa May.

Matabeleland's opponents are, probably, used to slightly better. Padania represent a North Italian region where the very name is synonymous with separatism to many from the Bel Paese. Their story is very different to Matabeland's, with Padania traditionally linked to the far right in Italy, the Lega Nord. Their call to split Italy in two is one that's ebbed and flowed over several decades. It's an association, naturally, that Padanian football team prefer to forget.

Should it happen, the establishment of a Padanian state would see the richest part of Italy engineer a split from the traditionally more laid-back south. The very concept of Padania - the area around the Po Valley - may well be as controversial in Italy as Matabeleland is in Zimbabwe, but they come from a very different world.

The Padanian side consists largely of players from the Italian Serie D, the first tier below Italy's fully professional ranks. They are reigning CONIFA European Champions, and expected to breeze through to the latter stages of the London tournament. In contrast to Matabeleland's exuberance, Padania's pre-match warm up, consists of the usual assortment of passing, stretching and keep ball. Their entire demeanour is almost boringly well-drilled and professional.

With the game underway, Padania reveal their slightly unusual strategy. They base the heart of their game around a slick, highly competent centre back, who orchestrates their best moments through long, looping balls around the pitch and an effortlessly classy touch.

The key man, Marius Stankevičius is a former Lithuanian international (and long-time resident of the Po Valley region of north Italy). The composed, long-haired defender has played near the peak of club football, including with Sampdoria, Lazio, Sevilla and Valencia. He's 37 now, but still conducts play with the effortless comfort of a man who knows he's the most capable on the field. Spraying his well-struck link-up passes around the pitch, he picks out players like captain Andrea Rota and Stefano Tignonsini, who have spent years kicking around the semi-professional tiers of Italian football, and feed eagerly on Stankevičius' obvious class.

The Matabeleland side contains only a handful of players of any real pedigree. Goalkeeper Notice Dube turns out regularly for struggling Zimbabwean second-tier side Makomo, in the north western town of Hwange. His home is best known as a stop off on the country's tourist trail, a quiet place that's home to ginormous industry in the Wankie Coalfield, and a break in the road on the way to Victoria Falls, or en route to a safari.

Fellow 'keeper Thandazani Mdlongwa and young forward Mduduzi Mpofu are both signed to tiny Zimbabwean club Victory United; most of the others haven't touched even the Zimbabwean league.

The Africans had hoped to include Cliff Moyo, a Zimbabwean international defender who plays professionally with Halifax Town, but Moyo couldn't commit, and besides, he'd have been pushing out a player traveling from Bulawayo, having trained for months with the team.

Inevitably, the tie is imbalanced. The Italians, clad in white shirts with stark red crosses pasted across the chest, are ruthless. They play a utilitarian brand of football, efficient and effective, caressing the ball into attacking positions.

There's an urgency, all bustling energy and naive one-on-one manoeuvres, to the Zimbabweans. They attack from the back, going for flicks through the legs, inventive angled passes and playful turns on the ball. Matabeleland play a brand of football that feels almost pre-strategy: a positive, flair-based game that's about showing your skill as much as winning a game. It's the game the Brazilians are famed for loving.

It doesn't work, of course. Defensive naivety is their biggest enemy, and while Matabeleland win over the crowd with their happy-go-lucky flair, Padania's exploitation of space and sharp finishing overwhelms the East Africans. Padania lead 5-0 at half time, and most of their glut of goals come from defensive errors.

Things are calmer in the second half. Padania do enough to win 6-1, former Venezia man Giacomo Innocenti comfortably the man of the match in the brutally efficient front line, grabbing two goals and two assists. As expected, the Italians, giants of the CONIFA World, take charge of Group C.

Matabeleland, though, are ecstatic at their scrambled late goal, and push hard for another in the closing stages. As both teams leave the field, the Matabeleland squad grin with emotion, and pause to take in the Sutton scenes. The Padanians trot straight down the tunnel, but the entire Matabeleland team divert to the side lines.

There are around 300-400 in the stadium by full time, and yet the Zimbabweans stroll the barrier's lengths, shaking hands with every member of the crowd, posing for photos, and pausing a little longer alongside the vibrant technicolour of their expat supporters in traditional dress. It's 20 minutes before they leave the field, to raucous applause and more than a few tears.

For Matabeleland, the journey to Sutton took 70 hours. The Zimbabwean side announced their arrival in 'CONIFA's brand of international football in a sunny, mismatched contest with a classy Italian side in suburban Surrey. They'd spent over an hour before kick-off handing out shirts, pre-ordered through a crowdfunding website in order to help pay for their flights. They played without fear.

Manager Justin Walley had seen something he liked. "We still think we can make it through," he said afterwards. "They're the strongest team in the group, and we were poor in the first half. Maybe a bit nervous. I'm expecting a lot more." Matabeleland have arrived, and brought their dreams with them. But being here is what mattered.

On the day the CONIFA World Football Cup kicks off in London, it's just over two weeks until the 2018 FIFA World Cup in Russia is set to follow suit. The superstars of World Football - Ronaldo, Messi, Iniesta and Kane - will play out a tournament already steeped in controversy before a ball has been kicked. Concerns incorporate hooliganism, human rights and corruption, and they're being talked about everywhere.

It's broadly accepted within the footballing community that everyone who reaches their country's international standard should get their shot at appearing at the World Cup, or at least in competing against some big-guns in the qualifiers. However unlikely it might be that they succeed, the likes of San Marino, Bangladesh, Gibraltar and Tonga all had their shot at glory in Russia, falling by the wayside as the field was narrowed to 32.

Of course, it's not as simple as 'every country gets its shot'. Nationality is an indistinct concept, and even at the less-arguable end of the spectrum, there are nations that FIFA chooses to ignore. The Federated States of Micronesia, for example, have an ongoing campaign for recognition. This was sparked in large part by CONIFA Director Paul Watson, who travelled to the island of Pompeii in an attempt to kick start first an island team, and then a fully-fledged national team. The Federated States are a country by almost any standard you care to name, yet their claims are falling on deaf ears due to the commercial realities of their isolation, and inter-island sporting in-fighting.

Monaco are another case; a top-tier French league team at club level, yet FIFA have no interest in their national entity. Tuvalu and Kiribati - the South Pacific island nations who align with CONIFA - can't get a look in with the main international body. Palestine only gained recognition from FIFA relatively recently, in 1998, as did Kosovo in 2014. Taiwan play Asian qualifying, but are forced to do so under the name Chinese Taipei, rather than their preferred name, under protest from China.

Then there are the less clear-cut cases, the ones FIFA can at least point to political recognition as a factor. Tibet, for example, could be viewed as a country without any land, or a people without any country. The Isle Of Man, who play with CONIFA under their Manx Gaelic name Ellan Vannin, don't get the same treatment as FIFA-accepted Gibraltar, though it's hard to see a clear distinction between the status of the two territories. As it stands, the Isle Of Man's players' shot at 'real' international football would be with England, though few born in the Isle of Man would claim to be English.

This only scratches the surface. There are countless regional identities, minority groupings, and other claims to nationhood spread throughout the globe and excluded from international sport, many with similar issues. CONIFA aims to be their umbrella.

CONIFA follows nine different selection criteria to broadly classify who is allowed to enter their organisation, and in turn attempt to qualify for their tournaments. Teams are classified as 'members' rather than 'nations', and their claims to identity range from slightly wishy-washy concepts like regional bio-identities to inarguable, broadly-accepted nationhood. Officially, CONIFA is loudly and pointedly apolitical, a claim the organisation's executive work hard to maintain. Naturally, at times that claim comes under intense scrutiny.

For most observers, there will be teams in CONIFA who evoke sympathy and awe, and others who evoke ire. They'll be some that cause confusion, and others whose lack of wider recognition is simply appalling. The games are ultimately about just one thing: promoting those who, in a sporting sense, want to show you who they are, but have all found themselves in the same difficult situation. They sit outside FIFA's fence, staring in.

The Birth of CONIFA: Reindeer Herding, Shirt Collecting and Sacrifice.

Even by the sometimes surreal and cloudy standard of sporting bodies, it takes only the briefest of chats with CONIFA's organisers to realise that what they've created is an odd and enthralling entity. In simple terms, it's a Swedish-based charity with no paid employees and a membership made up almost entirely of entities struggling for their very sporting existence. It's also a very wide-reaching labour of love, founded in July 2013, and now has competing member teams drawn in from every continent bar South America.

The organisation's roots lie with a few determined people, individuals prepared to put their lives - and in some cases their wellbeing - on the line for an underdog vision of footballing grandeur. In its short lifespan, it's hosted three World Football Cups and two European Cups, often in difficult corners of Europe, and grown consistently along the way.

CONIFA is not the first organisation to try and bring together a series of fringe national football teams rejected by FIFA, but to date, it is certainly the biggest.

2005 and 2006 were a hotbed for quirky unrecognised tournaments. Enthralling German socialist football club St Pauli hosted the surreal FIFI Wild Cup in their Millerntor Stadium in 2006. The tournament, won by Northern Cyprus, also featured Greenland, Zanzibar and Tibet as well as a team representing their famously party-loving, left-leaning region of Hamburg.

Prior to the FIFI Wild Cup, the Hamburg district of St Pauli informally 'declared independence' from Germany in order to compete. The club's fanbase are one with distinct anarchist tendencies and have become renowned for flying the skull and crossbones at every home game. Those in attendance cheered for Tibet even after they had been comprehensively eliminated, learnt that the Greenland side normally has to make do without grass, and got behind a Zanzibar side managed by a local as part of a bizarre reality TV show.

Amongst other, similar organisations, one long running example, is the 'Island Games'. Featuring the likes of the Guernsey, Jersey, Bermuda, Gotland and the Isle of Man, the event has been running since the late 80s, every two years. Its previous competitors include two countries now recognised by FIFA, Gibraltar and the Faroe Islands.

Things haven't always been so throwaway, or so specific, of course. The NF Board (New Football Federations Board), a precursor to CONIFA, hosted the UNPO Cup for Unrecognised Nations and People in 2005 in The Hague, The Netherlands, with South Pacific side South Moluccas seeing off Chechnya in the final.

The same organisation later expanded to create the VIVA World Cup (not an acronym, but a reference to the French verb 'to live'). That tournament ran for five cycles between 2006 and 2012, growing from three competitors at the first event (from which South Cameroons had withdrawn at late notice, due to visa issues), to a nine-team tournament by its conclusion.

The VIVA World Cup had plenty of playful approaches to football, including that some games during the 2008 tournament were played under the Swedish midnight sun. The hosts of that edition, Sápmi, had hammered everyone first time out in 2006, including a 21-1 final win against Monaco, but met their match in a new non-FIFA powerhouse, North Italian separatists Padania, come 2008. A certain Per-Anders Blind, who you will meet shortly, refereed at the event. The final, between Padania and Arameans Suryoye, an ancient Syrian ethnicity, saw the Italians triumph 2-0.

At the 2012 event, a popular television broadcaster in Iraq, Al Iraqiya, showed much of a tournament won by home side Iraqi Kurdistan. An impressive 22,000 people (3,000 more than the official maximum capacity) attended the host's final against Northern Cyprus, at the Franso Hariri Stadium in the town of Erbil. Erbil had been the site of several Iraq War massacres less than a

11

decade before. The home team's 2-1 victory saw them win the Nelson Mandela trophy.

Northern Cyprus initially refused to take part in the VIVA competitions, and instead created their own spin-off, the ELF Cup, persuading a number of other teams to compete with them. It's unclear why the split came about. The NF-Board claim that the newly elected Turkish Cypriot government of Ferdi Sabit Soyer insisted on restricting which teams could and could not take part in order to head off potential political arguments. Northern Cyprus in turn claimed that the NF-Board made unreasonable financial demands.

The Turkish Cypriots have long been viewed as a powerhouse of this particular brand of football, in part due to a history of playing more conventional national teams, including competing against Saudi Arabia and Turkey. After the non-FIFA giants returned to the fold for the VIVA World Cup's last edition in 2012, that final loss to Iraqi Kurdistan was their first ever defeat as a national team in a non-FIFA tournament.

By the time of the 2018 World Football Cup in London, CONIFA was firmly established as NF-Board's replacement. The organisation had grown to an unprecedented 46 sides, 16 of whom qualified to play at the finals, hosted by Somali minority Barawa in London. Their history, though, has also been a struggle. Here's a stroll through the journey so far...

CONIFA Is Born

CONIFA founder and President Per-Anders Blind came into what he calls the 'non-FIFA World' in 2006, due to his Sápmi heritage. Sápmi (commonly referred to as Lapland in English) is a traditional northern Scandinavian area, stretching across Norway, Finland, Sweden and the north-western corner of Russia. The Sami people of Sápmi are most commonly associated with reindeer husbandry, though they also have a rich cultural history incorporating unique clothes, tools, music and quirky-looking raised storehouses.

The group consists of approximately two million people, who have several of their own languages (some of which are incomprehensible to each other), their own parliament (in Norway) and several democratic councils. They've seen plenty of historical difficulties: various organisations are working extremely hard to undo years of culture repression that saw, for example, Sápmi people sent away to 19th-Century boarding schools in Norway designed to 'make them as Norwegian as possible', attacking their languages and culture along the way. Other laws have limited the size of Sami houses, and requisitioned Sami land.

The Sami would traditionally live specifically in vast open areas of the frigid north. Their existence, for generations, was a nomadic one, following the reindeer herds as they migrate along their natural pathways.

Of course, many Sami no longer work in these kind of areas, but the culture feels modern development heavily: reindeer get run down by trains, towns block migratory routes, and the instinctive navigation of animals is hit hard by the establishment of high-value mines, or the destruction of forests, as well as countless other problems generally related to human development on their land. The Sami, typically, are quite environmentally minded as a result, and many would prefer the option to continue with a lifestyle that far predates modern borders and development.

Due to his footballing background and refereeing qualifications, Blind was asked to follow a Sápmi side out to a VIVA World Cup in France as a match official, in 2006. He accepted, in part as flights, hotels and other expenses were all being covered. "I thought why not," he recalls. "But the whole tournament was a complete mess."

Four teams played at the 2006 VIVA World Cup, hosted by Occitania, a region that lies mostly in France, as well as taking in Monaco, part of Catalonia and part of Italy. It was poor quality:

Blind is only being slightly over the top when he jokes that the teams competing that year were "pulled from the streets."

Nevertheless, he returned to referee again in 2008, and started to get to know people around the organising committee. Using his experience as a professional business developer, Blind quickly got more involved, volunteering his time as an advisor and helping the organisation to grow.

The VIVA World Cup and organisers the NF-Board hung together until 2012, with those final games showing the potential, as Iraqi Kurdistan attracted 22,000 to the stands for what proved to be the finale hurrah. "It went from a banana tournament to a proper competition in that time," Blind remembers. "Things changed."

Blind is a serious man, not too different in demeanour to the men at the top end of mainstream international football. He often attends matches in a full suit and tie, networking and explaining, a picture of calm advocacy for the game, and his vision. Slightly slurring his S's in his near-perfect English, he's surprisingly open in giving his views on the organisation he founded, and freely admits to plenty of ongoing problems.

The old NF Board collapsed in February 2013 in Munich, due to in-fighting and a deadlock between voting members that arose from the structure of the Board's set up. The VIVA World Cup organisation's constitution gave all the founding members veto rights on all decisions, so the process only worked so long as everyone agreed. When they didn't, people and teams simply quit the organisation until only one person remained. They had lost faith.

Blind had been around a while, and had the ear of most of the teams as a result of his business management role. They started to come to him, and ask him to build something better. Aware of how messy the NF-Board had been over the past six years, he thought about it for a few months, simultaneously working on a new constitution. He intended to learn from the NF-Board experience, incorporating democratic principles, avoiding vetoes or excessive executive power, and structuring the organisation so as to serve the members.

Sascha Düerkop, later CONIFA's General Secretary, came on board, and the two travelled to the Isle of Man, gathered the teams together, and put forward their proposal. CONIFA was born, on the July 6 on island capital Douglas.

Düerkop, a German national, has a still more bizarre journey to involvement at CONIFA. "I collected football shirts," he explains, "and I still do. At some point I couldn't get any more shirts, as they are quite hard to source. I found out about teams outside FIFA, and contacted a couple of those. By coincidence, in 2013, one of the teams I had talked to, Cascadia, asked me to represent them at a meeting in Munich, as they couldn't make it over."

"I went, and it was a meeting of the predecessor of CONIFA, the NF-Board. The organisation collapsed at that meeting. Per-Anders asked me to help, as I was already in touch with a lot of the teams asking for shirts. I thought it would be a nice hobby. It's become quite a bit more."

There are a few principles that guide CONIFA, but one stands out. The concept of CONIFA is not political, though of course, the reality of keeping politics out is difficult, given the inevitably weighty views of those willing to represent an entity that may face political pressure at home, or not be broadly accepted. Blind views the organisation as a peace project, and while he accepts teams might have individual political agendas, those agendas are not supposed to make it to the pitch.

"I come from an indigenous people that were historically abused by the government, so it's deeply connected to me," he explains. "It's very important for these teams to be accepted, and given a global window. Many of them are neglected, abused, or forgotten. We give them a stage. It has a huge impact. They can be proud of their identity."

"We know it's stupid to say football is not political," Düerkop adds, "England being in FIFA is political, for example, because it's not a country. We try to keep political messages out of the stadium, but of course there is a lot of politics in some of these teams."

"The Chagos Islands are a good example," he continues. "They represent an Indian island group who were effectively forced to London by the British and American governments. They can't return, as the island is now a military base. They had to be sanctioned at the tournament in 2016."

The Chagos Islands residency issue is very much a live one. As recently as 2015, the Permanent Court of Arbitration at The Hague gave a verdict declaring that a marine protected area which the United Kingdom had established around the Chagos Archipelago in April 2010 was created in violation of international law. This ruling was important in the context of Mauritius' ongoing territorial claim over the islands.

"They had a banner saying 'let us return', and we couldn't allow that banner," Düerkop explains of the 2016 decision. "We'd have to do the same for a Free Tibet campaign, for example"

"It's not whether we agree about a political message. I personally might agree with Chagos, and maybe not with someone like Donetsk [a Russian-backed separatist state within the borders of the Ukraine], but that's not the point. The teams get the flag and the national anthem and that's it from the political side. Most of all, we're concerned with the teams and their cultural heritage."

The England 'not a country' controversy to which Düerkop refers, incidentally, applies equally to the other UK teams, too, and goes to FIFA's recognition criteria. While long convention sees England, Scotland, Wales and Northern Ireland compete separately as international entities, that's not technically what FIFA requires.

Austria and Germany initially objected to the four distinct teams, way back in 1904, and UEFA - FIFA's European feeder body - now tries to limit new members to UN recognised countries. That would mean a team representing the UK, not the individual region-states, in this case. Gibraltar were also only allowed into UEFA (and in turn FIFA) in 2013 as UEFA were not allowed to apply the new 'UN recognised country' requirements to an application already in process before their regulations were changed.

England, Wales, Scotland and Northern Ireland are allowed to continue playing football separately largely by convention, as the founder members of international football. This means the United Kingdom is now one of a very small number of UN-recognised countries that are not formally affiliated with FIFA in their own right.

That collection of countries that don't have FIFA membership is, in fact, a very small one. The UK is in an unlikely club of nine, alongside the Federated States of Micronesia, Kiribati, the Marshall Islands, Monaco, Nauru, Palau, Tuvalu and Vatican City. If not for a brief Great Britain team at the London 2012 Olympics and less than half a dozen representative games in the 40s, 50s and 60s, the UK would sit alongside The Marshall Islands as the only UN member country not to have fielded an on-the-record representative football team. Even for seemingly straightforward cases, then, football quickly reveals its politics.

Like CONIFA, the world body FIFA does claim to be apolitical, yet the demands it makes on the governments of the country that hosts its tournaments are notoriously substantial and weigh on the public purse, so that claim, perhaps, is arguably more difficult to sustain.

There are the countless allegations aimed at FIFA, of bribery, corruption and mismanagement, as well as the less direct consequences of the events, like the well-publicised deaths of mistreated workers in Qatar in the early build up to the 2022 World Cup. There's an entire other book in FIFA's exploits (in fact, several are already out there), but the short answer on football and politics is one most commentators have long known: yes, international football's political. Inherently so.

Nevertheless, there's a natural link between the two superficially competing entities, FIFA and CONIFA. For some teams, CONIFA is very much a stop-gap, one they're happy to be part of, but see as a stepping stone to establishing a FIFA team and going on to further recognition. Others have less lofty ambitions.

"Teams like Northern Cyprus and Iraqi Kurdistan are hoping to join FIFA, but play with us at the moment," Düerkop says. "The most ridiculous cases are places like Kiribati and Tuvalu. Kiribati have been trying to get into FIFA for 20 years. They've applied ten times, and they're not rejected, they just never get a reply."

Kiribati is an independent parliamentary democracy in the South Pacific with a population of 110,000. It's more populous than quite a few current FIFA members, from Montserrat (the smallest) to European minnows San Marino, Gibraltar and Lichtenstein. The collection of low-lying islands has been a full member of the UN since 1999, and is home to roughly a third of the number of people who live in Iceland, the smallest country to make a FIFA World Cup Finals to date, at Russia 2018.

"We've got some lawyers working for Kiribati on a pro-bono basis, because they need to get into FIFA," Düerkop says. "They just deserve to be there. It's probably money. It would cost a lot in development funds and travel money to include Kiribati in FIFA, but there wouldn't be any marketing gain. They probably can't formally reject them, so FIFA just don't reply."

"There are other problems for our teams," Düerkop adds, turning to a less sports-focused example. "Right now, the biggest problem is with Transnistria. Most teams have a border they can cross, but because of issues between Russia and the Ukraine, Transnistria can only go through Moldovan airports."

Transnistria is a largely autonomous separatist state located within the borders of Moldova, and home to over half a million people. The area was at the centre of a four-month territorial dispute in 1992, following the breakup of the USSR. That conflict, known as the Transnistria War, killed around 500 people, and involved local separatist forces, both Moldovan and Russian. Fighting is thought to have been triggered in part by ethnic Russians - who form a small majority in the area - having serious concerns about a potential amalgamation between Moldova and Romania, resulting in their marginalisation.

The UN considers Transnistria part of Moldova, though its status has never formally been resolved, and skirmishes still occasionally break out between Moldovan and Transnistrian forces. While formally not a country, the region has its own parliament, police force, passport, currency, constitution and postal system, and formally asked the UN for protection from – in their view -Moldovan aggression in September 2017.

"If the news gets out that a Transnistrian national team is traveling through Chisinau airport [Moldova], they'll get arrested and sent back, so they're not very active at the moment," Düerkop explains. "We have those problems at times, but usually they're anticipated." These kind of issues are not something CONIFA seeks out, but they are a natural consequence of what they do, and the organisation inevitably end up with these connections.

It's essential that all members are treated the same while they're with CONIFA, however, Blind explains. As well as having no emphasis on politics, the organisation places very little emphasis on how good - or otherwise - a side is at football.

That's something CONIFA likes to highlight as a key differential from FIFA, who are often accused of favouring the more marketable and successful nations. This has even led to existing FIFA members applying for membership of CONIFA instead, feeling neglected by the world governing body. CONIFA keeps the identity of these applications secret, and has encouraged them to go back to FIFA for the sake of their long-term future.

Of course, the idea that CONIFA itself might be apolitical, when it represents so many separatist states and minority groups, is only sustainable in so far as it comes to non-interference from the CONIFA executive. Given the lack of financial weight behind the volunteer head office, most of the political impact of CONIFA comes from the enabling of the sides themselves.

FIFA politics, in the form of marketing, even spread into CONIFA in the early days. The first CONIFA World Football Cup - a slightly clunky name gained after FIFA took issue with any use of the 'Football World Cup' branding, and suggested an alternative -

took place in Ostersund in Northern Sweden in 2014, with Blind's Sápmi side as hosts. It was preceded by another legal skirmish with FIFA, over the first proposed name for the organisation, CIFA. Judging by their actions, FIFA's primary issue with CONIFA was always potential damage to its brand.

For CONIFA's executive, the early days were an incredibly tough slog, with the first tournament taking a heavy personal toll for Blind in particular. The former referee, being based close to the tournament venue, was left to do much of the heavy lifting.

"I went all in, and I mean really, really all in," Blind recalls. "There were times when I could only eat one meal a day before the first tournament in Sweden. I couldn't afford to buy Christmas presents for my children, because I spent everything on CONIFA. I really burnt all the bridges behind me. There was only one way for me, and that was forward."

"It's difficult for CONIFA to mainstream our football," Blind explains of the strains on the organisation. "We have to prove ourselves. When it comes to sponsors and TV coverage and stuff, FIFA have a monopoly, and nobody wants to upset FIFA. We're always asked 'what does FIFA say, what does FIFA say'. Usually, when someone learns about CONIFA and understands our values, they don't leave. The way in can be a problem, though. A bottleneck."

"The main problem is definitely financial," Düerkop agrees. "It can't go on as a hobby like this forever, as you have to give it so much time. Kiribati would have had to pay $4,000 per ticket to get to London, so we weren't at all surprised they pulled out [the island team had been given entry ahead of nearby fellow competitors Tuvalu, who took their place]. We're an amateur organisation who don't pay salaries, but to plan this, we've had to work with the [British] Home Office and a consultancy that did the visas for the Olympics."

Indeed, visas have regularly been a substantial issue, both due to the often-politicised identities of the players, and the unrecognised nature of the tournament they travel to compete in. "I did them all myself in Sweden in three weeks," Blind recalls of the first tournament in Ostersund. "I managed to get them all in the end, but it was close. It was two minutes before the embassy closed."

Despite all the hassle involved in planning, the first CONIFA World Football Cup was a small affair. "It's a very small city, Ostersund, and there were mainly just about 100 Sápmi people at the matches," Düerkop remembers. "They were quite quiet, too. The atmosphere was really more amongst the teams, back at the start." That debut tournament was won by the French region County of Nice, a late call up to the event.

The crowds grew, but they're not the only measure of success. Part of the tournament is not really about football: most of the teams stay in the same place, and bonding off the pitch, from the post-tournament party to the discussions about CONIFA's direction, have become one of the major draws, especially for teams who travel knowing they're unlikely to progress all that far. Taking action, rather than just talk, is essential, and inter-team unity has helped keep things together when issues come up. Some of those issues have come close to causing diplomatic incidents.

Central Asian side Artsakh's appearance at the 2014 tournament caused the first big political drama, with formal complaints and a vocal protest from the Azerbaijani football association in Baku, directed at both FIFA and the Swedish government. CONIFA considered its principles and laid down a firm marker, refusing to revoke the team's invitation to the then twelve-team tournament.

The region of Artsakh is at the heart of a long-standing dispute between Azerbaijan and Armenia, and the Azerbaijani state saw the football team's appearance as a step towards separatism. Given the primary language and ethnicity of the region is Armenian, and even the flag echoes the Armenian banner, perhaps that view is not surprising.

Artsakh have since applied for FIFA recognition, with Samuel Karapetyan, head of their football association, arguing "We are convinced that recognition will come soon, because all the world is interested in establishing peace in this region. Sooner or later

Azerbaijan will recognize Artsakh, then we will participate not just in football but in every aspect of international life". They await their reply from FIFA, and continue to be a member of CONIFA, though they're yet to appear at another tournament.

In 2016, the second CONIFA World Cup was hosted by the region of Abkhazia, a semi-recognised state in the northwest of Georgia. The hosts took home the trophy, too. "Of course, Abkhazia tried to show to the world that they're a country, but that's not our business. We focus on respect," Blind explains.

"At the beginning of the tournament in Abkhazia the interest wasn't so high," he recalls. "But at the end it exploded. At the final, the stadium capacity was about 5,000 people. I think there were 11,000 people there, filling every corner. It was amazing."

Whether teams even appear at tournaments, though, remains a challenge. Two sides - Kiribati and Felvidek - were forced from the 2018 tournament after they were unable to raise the funds to travel. That only two sides failed to appear in London after qualifying was a substantial improvement on proceeding years. Karpatalya, a Hungarian minority group from The Ukraine, and Tuvalu, a South Pacific island, took their places, the former at only a month's notice.

Today, CONIFA claims to represent approximately 330 million people around the world through its teams. Every person within the organisation is a volunteer, yet they have risen to a status that enabled them to hold serious discussions with both Gibraltar and Kosovo, before both sides went on to join FIFA. Blind has even been involved in some sides' applications for membership to the world governing body. "Some of them just want to join FIFA, which is fine. It's nice. It's not for all of our teams, but it's what some want," Blind explained, showing complete apparent comfort with the idea.

Nevertheless, most of the time CONIFA is seriously ad-hoc. "It's a modern organisation; all our meetings are on Skype. There are no headquarters, it's all voluntary, but the high of taking part is amazing," Blind says. "When I was a referee, even at a banana tournament back in 2006, the people inspired me. It's about representing something bigger."

As part of their ethos, the organisation have created a system to include the poorer teams, too. "We always have something we call wildcards. These are for teams where perhaps they haven't qualified by skill, but there's a higher purpose, a social responsibility to let them in, like with teams like Tibet, or Tuvalu, who would never have a global opportunity otherwise."

Kiribati, for example, had been voted into the 2018 tournament by the members, having been unable to play qualifying games due to their isolated South Pacific location. They were intending to talk extensively about the country's overwhelming problems with climate change, as well as play football. When the Kiribati side couldn't afford the tickets, isolated not-so-near neighbours Tuvalu were given the slot instead.

The principle of admitting sides without the capacity for qualifying stands out next to other international tournaments where qualification is essential. CONIFA is a mixed bag: plenty of teams have to qualify, a few are given once-off special status. The idea is simple: access for those who could never get in otherwise, something that considers the very principles on which the whole concept was founded.

Sometimes, that results in very unequal matches. In 2014, a Darfur national team travelled to Sweden, with the side made up of players of Sudanese origin and drawn from a number of refugee camps in eastern Chad. At an obvious physical and technical disadvantage to the more established sides, Darfur lost their four games 20-0 (to Padania), 19-0 (to South Ossetia), 12-0 (to Artsakh) and 10-0 (to Tamil Eelam). Under the circumstances, CONIFA didn't really see the results as the point. Thirteen of the original Darfur players claimed asylum in Sweden at the end of the tournament.

"CONIFA is a family," Blind explains of the way such sides are incorporated into tournaments. "Everyone is equal, and we'll find a way to show that. We're only scratching the start line of a 100-yard journey."

Matchday One (part two): Colours of CONIFA, and Markers Laid Down

Tuvalu's bright blue, tangle-patterned shell suits and Matabeleland's black and orange jackets draw the eye as you enter the tight turnstiles into Bromley's rugged south London stadium. Unperturbed by their earlier thrashing, the Zimbabweans have taken to the pitch pre-match to dance and sing, surrounded by a loving media as they inject a rhythmic, swaying soul into the opening ceremony proceedings.

Tuvalu stand in a tight huddle, looking slightly overawed. Several of their players have a different body type to most of the athletes here, a kind of bulky, muscular frame unfamiliar on professional football pitches. The Tibetan squad wave their oversized, brightly coloured flags coated in Buddhist symbols, while the United Koreans In Japan unveil a massive banner in the twin scripts of Hangul (Korean) and Nihon-go (Japanese), a borderless image of the entire Korean peninsula filling one end. True to stereotypes, the Korean group serenely occupying themselves by gently picking the odd bit of loose trash from the 3G pitch.

In the crowd, a blue-suited, bearded man swoops a Cascadian flag vigorously overheard, while Hungarian diaspora sides Szekely Land and Karpatalya quietly look on, stern and athletic. CONIFA's first night arrives in a multicultural blaze of colour, its jet-lagged and match-tired participants strolling the turf wrapped in smiles.

The atmosphere around Bromley is largely one of quiet curiosity. There's a drone taking in the action overhead, and the colours of a plethora of London non-league sides coat those lining the barriers. Reading from the programme, Friday night drop-ins tell each other a little of the history of Kabylia or Abkhazia, while they sup their pints and await the action. Very few, it's clear, really know what to expect.

After a haunting, pitchy melody from a serene Tibetan musician, CONIFA President Per-Anders Blind takes the mic to address the crowd through tinny stadium speakers. He talks about struggles and representation, pride and passion. He welcomes the gathering crowd, and asks the sides to come together as one and treat the tournament as a celebration. The Swede's voice fluctuates with emotion, and the parading squads fade from the pitch to mingle in the crowd.

The opening ceremony, taking place on the evening of day one of the CONIFA World Football Cup at Bromley's compact Hayes Lane ground, features the last game of the tournament's opening day. This means Somali hosts Barawa and their opponents - Sri Lankans Tamil Eelam - have watched results pour in from around London. Fixtures in Sutton, Enfield, Haringey, Slough and Carshalton are already complete, making the pair the final sides to take to the field in the sixteen-team tournament.

This Barawa side, who represent the Somali diaspora in the UK, became an important symbolic representation of the coastal Somali town of the same name after terrorist group al-Shabab exploded a bomb in its crowded stadium two and a half months before CONIFA's kick off, killing five people. Barawa - also known as Brava - is little more than a small town, home to dusty roads and whitewashed houses, its stark poverty offset by white sand beaches and palm trees.

The town has come under the control of both al-Shabab and a local council in recent years. While the World Football Cup side is drawn from players based mainly in London, many of the players' families are back in Somalia, and caught up in the political crossfire of a dangerous region. The situation is very much a part of their lives.

The formal opening fixture has an added weight, then, especially for the hosts. Their opponents, Tamil Eelam, representing the Sri Lankan Tamil community, have also known the harshest of hard times. The Tamils were on the losing end of a civil war that ravaged Sri Lanka from 1983 until 2009. The war killed an estimated 150,000 people, and ended with the Tamil resistance dug into their final remaining piece of land, a shell-ridden north-Sri-Lankan beach, forced to surrender or back right into the sea.

When the game begins, it's the hosts Barawa who get off to a blistering start, driven forward by outstanding former QPR youth man Gianni Crichlow on the right wing. They play at a frantic pace, outmuscling their opponents and confidently passing into space.

Crichlow's moment comes when he charges down the right, takes down an angled ball, and fires a thundering lobbed shot over the head of Tamil goalkeeper Umaesh Sundaralingam and in off the back post from all of thirty yards out. Barawa go on to win 4-0, dismantling their opposition early on, and resilient until the end. Their players stay on the pitch until the floodlights turn off to explain to anyone interested what it all means to them. Their hopes, though, remain modest: to get out of Group A.

*

It's not possible to watch every game at CONIFA. With every team playing six games in nine days (and taking three well earned, dedicated days off), there's no time for the traditional gaps between games that are common at major football championships, and allow plenty of time for recovery, as well as time for television viewers to gorge on an extended footballing feast.

In London, though, there is online streaming from most of the key games, provided by sponsors Paddy Power, as well as handy highlights packages. It's become easier to catch up with all the CONIFA action than at previous tournaments, and coaches now have a chance to check out their typically obscure oppositions' performances from earlier in the tournament.

A few teams on the opening day are notably jetlagged, and unsurprisingly, the locally-based sides initially look the strongest.

In Barawa's Group A, two impressive looking squads battled it out in Sutton. Isle of Man side Ellan Vannin, dressed in a shirt that fades from red to orange, top to bottom, hit two top-class goals in seeing off a disorganised but physical and skillful Cascadia side, 4-1.

That game saw the North Americans fade fast after half time, having gone in 2-1 behind at the break. The Manx side's incredible third goal stood out: Sam Caine picked the ball up in his own half, made a tricky, meandering run, beating several Cascadian defenders, and hammered home from the edge of the box. Caine plays his football for Isle of Man champions St George's AFC, whose ground alternates between a football pitch and a campsite for the Isle of Man TT, the island's famous motorcycle race.

In Group B, Karapatalya caused the upset of the day, as they grabbed a 1-1 draw against one of the favourites, Northern Cyprus. The team of Hungarians from the Ukraine were late replacements in the tournament, and also left it late to equalise through Sándor István, who tucked away the rebound from a freekick. Northern Cyprus had dominated the early stages and led through Kenan Oshan's scrambled goal.

The other game in a tough group saw the holders comfortable, as reigning Football World Cup champions Abkhazia - a separatist region of Georgia - saw off Tibet 3-0 in front of the biggest crowd of the day, largely made up of passionate Tibet fans in Enfield. Abkhazia's squad featured Russian Premier League players like Anri Khagush (formerly of Rubin Kazan and BATE Borisov) and Anri Khagba. The inexperienced Tibetans limiting of the score to only 3-0 was a considerable achievement, given the side play their football in near isolation, typically competing only in regional tournaments in India.

Abkhazia man Khagush played in the Champions League back in 2009, memorably getting sent off against Real Madrid at the Bernabeu whilst playing for Belarus' biggest club, BATE. The Belarusian Champions lost that game 2-0 to a side featuring Ruud Van Nistelrooy, Raul and Arjen Robben. In contrast, none of the Tibetans had ever played professionally.

Over in Group D, 2016 runners up Panjab, representing the Punjabi speakers of a region of north west India and east Pakistan, laid down an eyebrow-raising marker. An 8-0 hammering of north Algerian Berber minority side Kabylia at their group-stage home base of Slough saw Kamaljit Singh and brother Gurjit Singh hitting four between them. Panjab found themselves immediately marked down as a major threat.

The South Asian side - representing the largest populace of any CONIFA entity - were ranked number one in CONIFA's official ranking system coming into the tournament, despite drawing most of their players from the English league's seventh and eight tiers. Goalkeeper Yousuf Butt stands out as a major asset, having spent his career in Scandinavia. The Canadian born stopper plays for Greve Fodbold in the Danish second division, and has been capped a dozen times for the Pakistan national team.

The opening day's only goalless draw came in the other Group D clash. Western Armenia and United Koreans In Japan were unable to break the deadlock in a defensive encounter that merits only an insipid two-minute highlights video, and shows the Armenians, in particular, to be an aggressive, physical side.

Matabeleland's group, Group C, saw Szekely Land - a Hungarian minority in Romania captained by former Hungary international Csaba Csizmadia - comfortable against a naive looking Tuvalu side, grabbing a 4-0 win. They could have had a few more, with Barna Bajko, captain of Romanian third tier club FK Miercurea Ciuc, hitting a hat trick. Tuvalu did create two clear sights of goal, but look shambolic in defence, providing little resistance to the powerful Szekely forward line.

In eight games on day one, the CONIFA World Football Cup produces 33 goals, and a whole lot of emotional moments, as several teams appear kitted out for the very first time. For most of these teams, their presence if the end of a journey, as well as a start.

Day one results (May 31, 2018):

Group A:
Cascadia 1 - 4 Ellan Vannin
Barawa 4 - 0 Tamil Eelam

Group B:
Karpatalya 1 - 1 Northern Cyprus
Abkhazia 3 - 0 Tibet

Group C:
Szekely Land 4 - 0 Tuvalu
Matabeleland 1 - 6 Padania

Group D:
Western Armenia 0 - 0 United Koreans In Japan
Panjab 8 - 0 Kabylia

Cascadia: "This Is Not An Independence Movement."

*Founded: 2013 **Record Win:** 6-0 v Tamil Eelam **Record Loss:** 4-1 v Ellan Vannin **Distance Travelled to London:** 4790 miles (7708 kms) **Home Capital:** Seattle, USA **Player Pool Playing In:** USA, Canada, England, Scotland, Denmark **CONIFA Ranking:** unranked*

It's three months until the CONIFA World Football Cup gets underway when I call Cascadia Association Football Federation President Aaron Johnsen hoping to explore the side's preparations. He sounds nervous and a little hazy, but also open and honest as he describes the struggles of Cascadia's planning across a dubious Skype line from the west coast of the US. It's fair to say things are a little behind.

"There is no team at the moment. We have still to confirm a coach," Johnsen says when I get a little ahead of myself and ask about the calibre of the players, and their progress. "We're hoping the coach we bring in will bring his own players. We're raising money, but we're going to have to think about players who can get to London on their own, with Cascadian connections. There have been a lot of delays. Really, we'd be looking at anyone who can add to a player pool at this point."

Things are problematic, and as a result, Johnsen is not overly optimistic about how things might go in London.

"Right now, we have about $7,000 we've pooled from shirt sales over the years," he continues, nodding to the Cascadian flag-based jersey that's become popular at Portland Timbers and Seattle Sounders games in American league the MLS. "To be fully funded for the tournament, we'd need about $35,000. We'd love to compete, but if we end up with a trophy... I don't want to say it would be a miracle, but it would be a little bit of a Hollywood ending."

I was starting to wonder if Cascadia were actually going to show up in London at all. Feeling brave, I asked. Johnsen said the chances were at about 75%, but his hesitant tone tells me that might be on the optimistic side. Part of the reason a team hasn't been formed is straightforward: Cascadia hadn't needed to qualify. Their status as the only North American representative at the time of London qualification - 'local' rivals Quebec re-joined CONIFA after the tournament qualifying cut-off date - meant Cascadia had got the right to play in London without ever playing a game. They were clearly woefully underprepared.

The idea of a Cascadian football team was first mooted shortly after the 2012 Olympics, following talk on US soccer forums. This led to the production of the popular early national shirt by the Cascadia Trifecta Facebook group, a page dedicated to the three major teams in the region, Vancouver Whitecaps, Seattle Sounders and Portland Timbers. It was a nice, imaginative, speculative and popular commercial venture, but at the time it didn't lead to anything approaching a team.

"In 2013 there was a call out on Twitter by a guy called Lenny Laymon," Johnsen says, of the moment the idea became public. "He said he was working on this Cascadia team idea, and about ten people turned up to that first meeting. We applied to the NF-Board [CONIFA's precursor] for membership at that time. We were just a bunch of fans of Portland, Seattle and Vancouver. Here we are, five years later, still trying to make things happen."

The concept of Cascadia is an interesting one, falling a little on the fringes of CONIFA's remit. It's based around the idea of a bioregion, an area bonded by its shared natural environment. A bioregion is usually enclosed by natural, environmental borders and shared natural atmosphere. That means river catchment areas, in Cascadia's case, as opposed to human-established lines on a map. The Cascadian ideal is aimed at bonding its population through shared connection to that environment.

Cascadia Now!, a website at the heart of the movement, defines the Cascadian region as "in many ways geographically, culturally, economically and environmentally distinct from surrounding regions. It's defined through the watersheds of the Columbia, Fraser and Snake River valleys. It is a place in the world with unique flora and fauna, topography and geology, and is comprised of interconnected ecosystems and watersheds." In Cascadia's case, the region's identity also stretches into social interconnection and political beliefs, too, with the idea acknowledged by both the US and Canadian governments.

There are differing interpretations of exactly where the region's borders sit, aside from being loosely defined as to the west of the Cascade Mountains in the Pacific Northwest. Approximately, Cascadia incorporates Washington State and Oregon (US) and British Columbia (Canada).

The region is home to a small but serious secessionist movement, albeit largely active on social media. Led by the Cascadian Independence Party, the movement is left-leaning and environmentally conscious, going heavily into progressive ideas like open source government, regional sustainability and local food networks. It has gained substantially more traction since 2010, and in particular in reaction to Donald Trump's election.

"It's a unique culture. It's more laid back than the rest of the country, and soccer is huge here," Johnsen explains of the area often singled out as American soccer's heartland. "It's easy to pick out someone from this area just by looking at them. The way we dress, the mannerisms. It's not necessarily about politics, but a home-grown attitude, keeping things local, and our culture. We started a team to represent our area in a sport we love."

Johnsen isn't joking about the unique culture. Portland, in particular, is famous for its quirkiness, which stretches to claiming their 'world's smallest park', Mill Ends Park, contains the only colony of leprechauns west of Ireland. They have a 21ft chocolate waterfall, a museum focusing solely on vacuum cleaners, a coffee shop centred around a coffin, and a vegan strip club. In that context, perhaps the rejection of mainstream sport in the area in favour of relatively unfashionable America soccer is not all that surprising.

The Cascadian movement also finds a lot of its routes in a kind of late hippiedom, with forest-loving locals around the region increasingly known for fighting development taking place in their forests, attempting to influence conventional American thinking, and pushing environmental agendas in general into the limelight.

The passion for football is most clearly born out in Portland, whose lively fans have gained a huge reputation in the MLS, and even in Europe for their boisterous, manic support of the Timbers, another community-focused entity. In the Timbers' stadium, the traditions of the area in general filter in. There's a ritual, for example, of sawing a chunk off a huge log every time the home team score a goal. That means the crowd always features a man with a chainsaw, a hard hat and a mounted tree trunk over a foot thick, representing 'Timber Town'.

Despite their being no Major League Soccer players available, as CONIFA's tournament sits right at the heart of the American season, the late-notice Cascadian side does end up looking surprisingly strong. James Nichols - coach of seventh tier English team Kendal Town - is appointed manager. Though the pictures that emerge showing his team departing Seattle feature so few athletes they look more like they're set to play a five-a-side contest, local recruitment has gone well.

The first major coup is the recruitment of recently retired former MLS star James Riley. The right back, who left Colorado Rapids in 2015, was once on the cusp of the American national squad. He's quickly appointed captain: local media have worked hard to sell Riley's agent the idea of the former Seattle Sounders' star lifting the trophy in Cascadian colours, and the rangy player - also director of the MLS' Player Relations group - has been talked around.

Next came the support of Wolves scout Jack Thorpe, fresh from seeing his own side return to English football's top table after a magnificent second-tier season. Thorpe started to work on building a local squad, pulling together a selection of players with Cascadian connections from across the UK to add to the small traveling contingent. Riley's inclusion, alongside the prospect of international football, became a major draw.

Elgin City's Canadian age-group international Calum Ferguson and ex-Manchester United squad player Joshua Doughty (born in Vancouver) come on board. They're joined by players from Barnet and Danish second division club Nykøbing FC, as well as a host of non-league youngsters plying their trades in the English amateur tiers. There are half a dozen from American colleges and smaller Cascadia-region clubs. The result is a big, physical side, one that's extremely young, technically proficient and defensively strong.

Later, the Cascadian media following let slip that the team had never met, let alone been on the same pitch, until the day before the tournament. The American contingent landed and trained with their new teammates for the first time all on the same day, the Wednesday before kick-off, fighting jet lag along the way. The following day, they took to the pitch in the tournament's opening day as virtual strangers. They lose, badly, 4-1 to Ellan Vannin, but look surprisingly good in the process. They'll have to come together quickly, though as at CONIFA, the games come thick and fast.

Cascadia are one of few sides with a genuine travelling support at the tournament in London, with a number of media organisations and followers making their way 'across the water'. Their flag - the 'Doug Flag', featuring a fur tree and shades of white, green and blue, representing snow, mountains and sky - is a common sight around the barriers. Several of their games feature information stands with passionate representatives touting the bioregional concept and Cascadian beliefs.

There are printed information pages and brightly coloured pins, shirts and scarfs, and the politicised handful of travellers are happy to engage on all things Cascadian. It quickly becomes clear how serious the concept is to the group: they unquestionably see themselves as primarily Cascadian, rather than American or Canadian.

One fan becomes one of the enduring symbols of the tournament. With his beard, twirling moustache, sharp blue suit and

Cascadia pin, he waves a large Doug flag attached to a sturdy tree branch over the terraces at every Cascadian games.

There are some extremely serious secessionist movements within CONIFA, but despite the passionate fan base, Cascadia's soccer team seems to lean the other way. Born in part on social media, they're ultimately about pride, and let their Twitter account stake their claim in the form of a quiet disclaimer. It reads simply 'Cascadian soccer. This is not an independence movement.'

"The independence movement is definitely a thing," Johnsen tells us, "but we're not part of it. It's a bit of a left wing, anti-Trump thing at the moment. Cascadian independence won't happen, and it's not what we're about. This is just about asserting our regional identity and getting it out there. And about having fun."

The Pre-London Years: A Quick Glance at the Sporting Side of CONIFA's First Four Tournaments.

You're probably new to CONIFA. Most people are, so what takes place in London might require a little context. As you've already learnt, London wasn't the start. In fact, the 16-team tournament - CONIFA's largest to date - is the fifth they've managed to pull together since forming in 2013. While every one of those tournaments so far has taken place in Europe, they have spread to diverse and CONIFA-appropriate corners of the continent, meeting a fair bit of opposition along the way.

London, as a modern metropolis where the primary claim to 'independence' seems to be a jokey one rolled out in response to Brexit, is very much an exception to the tournament-hosting rule. The other four tournaments had more obvious links to the CONIFA entity that hosted them, but 2018 hosts Barawa had no real prospect of bringing the tournament to its unstable corner of Somalia, where a football match was recently bombed. Besides, the team had formed in London.

Broadly speaking, the development of CONIFA has been a messy process, riddled with team withdrawals and financial and political difficulties, yet the organisation has consistently expanded, and is now approaching 50 members. In four different Championships prior to London, there were three different winners; Padania won, and later retained the European Championship, while the three World Football Cups have ushered in three different champions.

Here, in brief, is the story of those tournaments so far...

2014 CONIFA World Football Cup: Hosted by Sápmi in Ostersund, Sweden.

Participating teams (12): Iraqi Kurdistan, Padania, South Ossetia, Sápmi (hosts), Arameans Suryoye, Artsakh, Occitania, County Of Nice, Abkhazia, Darfur, Ellan Vannin, and Tamil Eelam.

Other qualifying teams (2): Zanzibar (withdrew due to visa problems), Quebec (withdrew, having chosen to withdraw from non-FIFA football to chase CONCACAF recognition, a move that required the team to only play FIFA recognised opposition. Having failed, they later successfully reapplied to CONIFA)

CONIFA's debut tournament struggled to come to fruition, hosted by Per-Anders Blind and his Sápmi Scandinavian ethnic minority, in the far northern Swedish town of Ostersund. Ostersund later became known for English manager Graham Potter pulling the amateur side from division four to the Swedish top tier, where they play summer-season football - the only type possible in a town of 50,000 dubbed 'ice city'.

Sápmi had previously hosted the NF-Board tournament, and so had some familiarity with CONIFA-style football, making them a natural choice, perhaps, especially with one member of the executive located suitably locally.

The debut CONIFA tournament took place in a 'four groups of three' format, with the top two from each group progressing to the knock-out stages. Padania set the early pace, with a brave Darfur team made up of refugees plucked from their camps in central Africa proving the whipping boys, losing their two group-stage games 20-0 and 19-0 to Padania and South Ossetia respectively.

County of Nice - a late replacement call-up to the tournament after Zanzibar were forced to pull out - lost early to Isle of Man side Ellan Vannin, but the French region started to make a real impact in the knockouts, dispatching favourites Padania and their group rivals Ossetia to make it to the final.

Three of the four quarter finals went to penalties, with only County Of Nice grabbing a normal time win. Next, Ellan Vannin come from a goal down to beat Arameans Suryoye in the semi-final, 4-1, joining the French side in the decider.

The Manx outfit were slight favourites going into the final, especially given they'd already beaten County of Nice 4-2 in the group stage, with Calum Morrissey scoring a hat trick.

The final was a cagier affair, ending in a 0-0 draw before County Of Nice scored all five of their penalties to be crowned champions. Darfur, rank outsiders departing from shoddy camps in the desert to take part, never got within ten goals of an opponent, but they'd done something more important: set down a marker in terms of CONIFA's ambitious reach.

2015 European Football Cup, hosted by Szekely Land in Debrecen, Hungary:

Participating teams (6): County Of Nice, Padania, Szekely Land (CONIFA tournament debut, hosts), Felvidek (debut), Ellan Vannin, Romani People (debut).

Other qualifying teams (7): South Ossetia, Abkhazia, Northern Cyprus (each refused visas), Monaco, Sápmi, Nagorno-Karabakh (a.k.a Artsakh), Franconia (each withdrew for financial or organisational reasons).

The tiny debut regional CONIFA event, the first European contest, turned out to be a bit of an organisational nightmare. The tournament had initially been awarded to Ellan Vannin, to take place on the Isle of Man, with the early blueprints showing some games to be played in the South East of England. The English groups games would be followed by semi-finals and a final in Douglas, the island's capital. Logistical issues regarding venues and travel arrangements proved too much for hosts Ellan Vannin, and while their side still took part, they ultimately stepped aside from their flagship role completely.

The tournament moved to Szekely Land, in Hungarian-Romania, and then, having faced objections and potentially visa issues locally, moved to Hungarian capital Budapest. It ultimately settled on Hungary's second city Debrecen, the fourth and final mooted venue. Team participation was equally messy: while six teams ultimately turned up to play the tournament, a further seven had withdrawn at various stages. Franconia, Monaco, Sápmi and Nagorno-Karabakh (also known as Artsakh) were followed out of the tournament by South Ossetia, Abkhazia and Northern Cyprus for reasons varying from visa problems to being unable to raise finances. It's likely the latter three's connections with Russia and Turkey had not gone down well with the Hungarian government.

When things did finally get underway in Debrecen, County Of Nice saw off the two Hungarian-linked teams, Szekely Land and Felvidek, to win their group, while Padania edged both of their games to come out on top, too. The pair were joined by Ellan Vannin and Felvidek in the semis. Unlike the first tournament, there had been no whipping boys.

After County Of Nice and Padania both won their semi-finals, the north Italian side beat the 2014 World Football Cup holders in the final 4-1, comfortably avenging their defeat to Nice a year earlier. Ellan Vannin grabbed third on penalties. The three sides with previous CONIFA tournament experience from 2014 grabbed the top three places, a strong hint at something that's proven true at a FIFA level was transferring to CONIFA, too: success at an international level correlates closely with a team's level of long-term international experience.

2016 World Football Cup, hosted in Abkhazia, a semi-autonomous region of Georgia

Participating teams (12): Padania, Abkhazia (debut), Raetia (debut), Somaliland (debut), Iraqi Kurdistan, Chagos Islands (debut), Panjab (debut), United Koreans In Japan (debut), Northern Cyprus (debut), Sápmi, Western Armenia (debut), Szekely Land.

Other qualifying teams (3): Ellan Vannin (withdrew on the advice of the UK foreign office), Romani People, Aymara.

The decision to award the 2016 tournament to Abkhazia was a loud and purposeful statement, one made in direct response by the CONIFA executive to the refusal of Hungary to award Abkhazia and South Ossetia's players visas at the 2015 European tournament. The choice was made in the direct aftermath of the 2015 event, and while it wasn't the most accessible of locations, Abkhazia's hosting role was designed to show backing for all members, rather than play political favourites.

The boldly chosen location presented problems for some teams, in particular Ellan Vannin, who chose not to travel after the UK government indicated that they perceived substantial risks in traveling to the Russian-backed separatist region. However, with no fewer than eight of the 12 sides debutants, and the arrival of traditional non-FIFA powerhouse Northern Cyprus, the Abkhazian tournament was a step up for CONIFA. The one disappointment was the tournament did miss out on what would have been a first ever South American participant when indigenous Andean side Aymara pulled out.

Hosts Abkhazia were causing a storm locally, attracting huge crowds to the Dinamo Stadium in Sukhumi, where they hammered the Chagos Islands 9-0 and edged past Western Armenia to win their three-team group.

Northern Cyprus opened with a win against the ever-present Italians Padania, but both progressed, and newcomers Panjab, driven forward by the Purewal brothers made waves in Group D. Iraqi Kurdistan also looked strong.

The semi-finals saw four powerful sides left in the tournament: Panjab surprised everyone by edging past experienced Padania 1-0 to reach the final, and hosts Abkhazia finally saw off the Turkish Cypriot challenge to join them. In a final shown on national television in Abkhazia, an 88th minute equaliser from Ruslan Shoniya, and a sudden death penalty win coming after eight penalties each saw the hosts take the title. The final was played out in front of a crowd of thousands more than could officially fit in the stadium, with an attendance of 11,000. CONIFA was arguably at its highest ebb.

Aymara, who were unable to make the tournament, are an interesting footnote. Now withdrawn from CONIFA, the Andean indigenous people from Bolivia, Peru, Chile and Argentina are the only South American side to even get so far so as to join CONIFA to date. While Aymara sides have played in The Campeonato Nacional de Futbol Pueblos Originarios (Copa ANPO), a football tournament for indigenous people in South America, they never formally took part in a CONIFA contest, having been invited in 2016 as a continental wild card.

2017 CONIFA European Football Cup, hosted by (and in) Northern Cyprus

Participating teams (8): Northern Cyprus, Abkhazia, South Ossetia, Felvidek, Padania, Karpatalya (debut), Ellan Vannin, Szekely Land.

Other qualifying teams (3): Sápmi, County Of Nice, Occitania.

As one of the powerhouses of CONIFA football, Northern Cyprus' hosting of the 2017 European tournament also brought in a rare moment of stability for CONIFA. While three teams did withdraw from the tournament (an improvement on the early days, but still a withdrawal rate of nearly 40%), there was only one debutant at the island contest, hosted across four grounds in the less-visited half of the stony, clear-watered Mediterranean island.

For the first time, the tournament moved to conventional four-team groups, which meant more games per team. The hectic new 'three group games in four days' format for the tournament was also established.

The quality of the teams involved led to things becoming more competitive: aside from an 8-0 thrashing of South Ossetia by the hosts, only one other group game - also a South Ossetia defeat - was won by more than two goals.

Northern Cyprus and World Football Cup holders Abkhazia progressed from group A, where they faced consistent Italians Padania and Szekely Land in the semi-finals. Northern Cyprus then saw off Szekely Land 2-1 in their semi-final, while Padania went on a well-timed run of penalty wins. The North Italians had been threatening to win a title since CONIFA got underway four tournaments earlier, in 2014, and finally got one. First, they beat Abkhazia 6-5 on penalties, and then their Cypriot hosts 4-2 in a shootout in Nicosia to bring the trophy back to Northern Italy in a tense encounter.

Hell yes, it's political.

Sport isn't political, we're often told. Or at least it tries not to be. But let's be honest, it doesn't work. From the anthem-kneeling protests of modern-day American footballers to racism protests at the Olympics via that post-Apartheid South African rugby squad, there are countless times through history when politics and sports have been intimately linked.

That's also true of football. It's especially true of football at an international level. Let's start with a few clear-cut examples.

In July 1969, El Salvador and Honduras played the second of two World Cup qualifiers in the former's capital San Salvador, a city famed for its gangs, widespread armed security, and high murder count. The first game in June had been won 1-0 by Honduras, the earlier contest was followed by extensive fighting between the two country's fans.

At the return leg, El Salvador beat their neighbours by a resounding 3-0 score line, and once again riots broke out around the ground between supporters. In the aftermath, El Salvador alleged the match (and the Honduras' defeat) led to the expulsion of over 10,000 of their citizens from their neighbour and back to El Salvador.

In retaliation, the El Salvador government severed diplomatic ties the same day as a playoff game between the two - the third time the pair had played inside a month. That game was played in Mexico City, for obvious reasons, and led to a 3-2 win for El Salvador, with the escalation of military conflict already underway back home.

In truth, the break out of war between the two countries was about a lot more than football, but the three vital games had proven a catalyst. The countries were falling out over issues like land reform, and the immigration of citizens from the highly-populated El Salvador into their relatively empty, larger neighbour Honduras. Nevertheless, football played into the escalation, and the war became known as 'The Football War'.

43

Political influence happens across entire waves of club and international football, too. When Muammar Gaddafi still ruled over Libya with an iron fist, for example, many were appeasing his regime in the name accessible and affordable Libyan oil. His son Al-Saadi Gaddafi wanted to be a footballer. While competent, most would agree Gaddafi junior was not an outstanding footballer, but his familial status, as the son of a notoriously difficult leader, put the local league in an awkward position.

For reasons likely closely linked to the identity of his father, Gaddafi was drafted into a career at two different Tripoli clubs, where the referees would typically rule heavily in his favour, and a law allegedly forbid the in-stadium announcement of any player but him by name. Teammates and opponents were said to fear doing anything that would make Gaddafi look less than outstanding. Suddenly, the integrity of an entire national league had been compromised by a single player.

Astonishingly, Al-Saadi was soon made captain of the Libyan national team, and later moved on to a series of Italian clubs, with links quickly drawn up by a suspicious media between the chosen sides and their owners' possible interests in Libyan oil.

Perugia (where Gaddafi played for a few minutes), Udinese (where he somehow won a few minutes more out on field) and Sampdoria (where he never made the pitch) all signed the general's son. All three played in Serie A, the top tier of the widely-heralded Italian leagues, at the time. The Colonel's son was said to employ disgraced Olympic sprinter Ben Johnson as his fitness coach and Diego Maradona as a consultant, as he power-tripped his way to fulfilling many a childhood dream.

Then there's the incredible story of the Eritrean national team, who travelled to away games on several occasions and simply never came back. The isolated and often difficult country sent a representative team to Angola in 2007, and six players chose to claim asylum rather than go home again. Two years later, twelve more defected in Kenya. In 2012, an entire team and several staff - 17 people in total - departed for an away game in Uganda and never returned home. It happened again in 2015, with ten players seeking asylum in Botswana.

The defections, of course, are reflective of the shocking conditions inside the north-east African country, with problems so substantial that the usually relatively-heralded position of member of the international football team became simply a convenient vehicle for players to escape the country.

Things got so bad that in 2008 and 2010, the government even required security from its own players to prevent them from absconding when they arrived at away games. The measure did seem to temporary stem the flow, and saw some players later say they feared for their family had they run.

Even players from Eritrea's outstanding club team, Red Sea FC, have fled during away African Champions League games. The problem's not unique to football (several athletes have followed the same course), but it has become a strange fact of life at the top of Eritrean soccer, where reaching international level comes with the chance at a very different kind of better life.

There's very little nuance to these cases: they're overtly political. Let's not pretend, either, that the politics impacting heavily on football is restricted to poorer or less established clubs and countries. FIFA's list of demands on the governments of those countries looking to host a world cup, for example, is becoming increasingly notorious. Chicago and Vancouver both dropped out of the 2026 North American bid before the US/ Canada/ Mexico triple-bid won the hosting rights, because the financial demands being placed on the cities were seen as unacceptable.

These FIFA requests (they're really demands, at least if a bid is to be taken seriously) include an exemption from the country's labour laws for those working on the World Cup, an exemption from local tax for a number of different entities, non-beneficial lease agreements on local stadiums (i.e., no benefit to the local stadiums), and the hosts to foot essentially the entire bill for the tournament. Those costs include onerous security expenses to not taxing the tournament, or even its related events.

The list, brazenly published online by FIFA for potential bidders, essentially makes political interference and high demands on taxpayer money a prerequisite for hosts. It's a set of demands that often gets lost behind the local excitement generated by winning bidders, but not always. In such a demanding context, it's entirely unsurprising that even developing yet football-obsessed country like Brazil ultimately ended up with mass protest against the tournament, and especially its cost, when they hosted in 2014.

Russia in 2018, of course, came with an entirely different set of political issues, largely around corruption and state discrimination. The 2022 tournament in Qatar has still bigger difficulties. At the time of writing, three years before the tournament, most estimates already put the construction worker death count in the Middle Eastern state in the low thousands.

Both UEFA and FIFA also play politics in their draws, though there's a strong argument that it's done in the general interest. Russian and Ukrainian sides couldn't draw each other in the Champions League at one point, to avoid potential flashpoints. Kosovo and Serbia, Russia and Georgia, Spain and Gibraltar and Armenia and Azerbaijan have at various times been kept apart in 21st century international qualifying draws. Mainstream football bodies, in effect, tacitly admit they have to account for politics in their actions.

CONIFA's politics is in its nature: the very fact that you're the organisation that allows teams like Abkhazia, Tibet and Northern Cyprus to play football is reason enough for some people to find things problematic. What there certainly isn't is death, discrimination, demands made on governments, requirements that teams be kept separate, or even games flooded with aggression because of the conflicting ideas of two countries.

Things are, generally, played in a very positive spirit. The fans don't mob each other, the protests are modest (and generally in academic - or at least written - form), and the players, playing for nothing but pride, look ecstatic to be there. Plus, the organisation itself doesn't get involved. Politics, even in the narrow arena of football, takes vastly different shapes. Despite perceptions, CONIFA has to date been quite moderate.

Matchday 2: Hungarian Passion, and the Wembley Contrast...

Inside Haringey Borough's compact Coles Park ground in North London, the presence of a large number of boisterous Hungarians is immediately obvious. With green, red and white flags draped over swathes of the meshed pitch-side barriers, they're a loud, boozy presence on the Saturday afternoon touchline, clutching banners tagged with lines like 'Székely Magyar' (Transylvanian Hungarians) and 'Mezomagyar London' (London greater Hungarians).

Most are bulky, tattooed and intimidating in a way common to lads at football, but I take a deep breath, and decide to dive into the thick of things. I try to persuade a flag-clutcher with intoxicating beer breath to give me his thoughts on the concept of the region his team hail from, Székely Land. I know immediately that my question is too 'academic' for beer and football, and I'm quickly proven right. I'm yet to finish introducing myself when his friend ducks down beside me, and starts fiddling with my shoes.

I'm wearing an old pair of illuminous blue five-a-side Sondicos, complete with a growing split along the join of the sole and the synthetic toe cap. They're within days of the trash can, so I'm not overly concerned about what he's up to. It soon become clear he's trying to remove a part of my laces.

My new friend thinks he's being subtle. He isn't, but I decide to plough on anyway. I keep half an eye on the lighter flame that's now burning through the over-sized black lace hanging from my on-their-last-legs trainers, as I chat to his overly-loud partner in crime.

"We are Hungarian, like Székely land," a rowdy man in the green and white stripes of 29-times Hungarian champions Ferencváros tells me. "We live now in London, but we don't forget home." He pauses to swig from a can of beer he seems to have smuggled through the gate. "You shouldn't stay near Hungarian ultras," he continues. "We will troll you." Seconds later, I feel the firm yank of a part of my shoelace being plucked from its scalded roots. The second Hungarian rises sniggering from his crouch by my feet.

"He took this," the first guy says, pointing, and unable to hold in his laughter, as he indicates the six inches of cheap, dirty, half-melted shoestring hanging between his friend's two fingers. "I told you we will troll you," he adds.

The pair ask, somewhat belatedly, if they can use the string to attach their flag to the pitch side barrier alongside the rest of the green, white and red display. I choose the only option that makes any sense, nod, and shrug. Then the spokesman, after a break to translate for his friend, leans back into me.

I'm trying not to wince at the heady hit of stale midday beer on his breath as he attempts to whisper - at achingly substantial volume - in my ear. "In here," he says, pointing at a crammed-to-bursting bag beneath his feet where I'm expecting to see quite a few more beers.... "In here, we have the flares. So many flares."

With that, and a snigger, he turns and heads off into the crowd, leaving his bag of pyrotechnics propped against the stadium-side barrier. The remnants of my shoelace now hangs from the pitch-side hoardings beside his abandoned, poorly hung flag. A few metres down the sidelines, the chants have started, and a handful of people draped in three-coloured flags are dancing boisterously along.

Székely Land are, in essence, a product of the Austro-Hungarian Empire. The name originally referred to the autonomous seats of power situated in an area right in the heart of Romania, in the Transylvania region, and occupied by the Székelys, a minority group who are usually considered to be Hungarian. The area, known as Ținutul Secuiesc to Romanians, still has a Hungarian majority right up to the present day.

Székely Land became part of Romania in 1920, yet calls for independence or self-governance have been consistent since, and have become more and more vocal in recent years. Székelys are famously sentimental about their land, which is largely rural, sporting plenty of its own traditions, it often appears to outsiders to be more old-fashioned and slow-paced than much of the surrounding area. The blue and gold Székely flag is commonly flown from buildings, many of which still contain the traditional decorative, wood-carved frames and features of Székely Land's old architecture.

The region is not new to controversy in modern-day footballing circles. When Hungary played Romania in Bucharest in 2013, the pair contesting a qualifier for the 2014 World Cup, a number of Hungarian fans were arrested for disturbing the public order. One of the issues cited was their waving of Székely flags towards their Romanian counterparts.

Hungarian sources have also reported that Székely region team Sepsi OSK - newly promoted to the Romanian top flight in 2017/18 - were vocally subject to calls to 'go home' from fans of traditional powerhouse Dinamo Bucureşti at an away game during their first Romanian Liga 1 season.

Politics and football have come to echo each other to some extent in the region in recent years, and as well as the outright separatist element of Székely people, there are ongoing pressures to give the region improved levels of autonomy within Romania.

Such calls largely lean on the historical context of that past semi-autonomous status, previously allowed behind the Iron Curtain under the heading the 'Magyar Autonomous Region' between 1952 and 1968. Calls for independence have grown in volume since the election of right-wing Hungarian President Viktor Orban, but have rarely been out of the local news in the region since the fall of the Communist bloc in 1989.

Most recent amongst the shouts for Szekely autonomy, the various strongly Hungarian-connected regions in Romania - there are others - unified to make some vocal claims for independence early in 2018.

The three Hungarian-led Romanian parties – the Democratic Union of Hungarians in Romania, the Popular Hungarian party in Transylvania, and the Hungarian Civic Party – announced a common position in Cluj Napoca, Transylvania's biggest city, with the intent of asserting pressure on the Romanian government. The three parties share 30 seats in Romania's parliament, a significant and at times influential 10% of the Parlamentul Românei's total numbers.

In Cluj, the group said they wish to negotiate three types of autonomy – territorial, local/ administrative and cultural.

"These three types of autonomy have to be discussed as soon as possible, even in 2018, with the Romanian majority and translated into legislation," said Kelemen Hunor, leader of the Democratic Union of Hungarians in Romania, the largest of the parties.

He argued that while autonomy would help to preserve the ethnic identity of the Hungarians in Romania, it would also "contribute to the development of society in Romania" more generally, adding that in other areas it "has worked and is still working, and is the key to development." Wales and Scotland's regional parliaments and identities are commonly cited as possible models for areas like Szekely Land to follow.

As well as their simple strength in democratic numbers, the Hungarian nationalist parties have obtained a surprisingly strong position of influence in the Romanian parliament. In 2018, their votes are required to push through the ruling socialist government's policies, giving the groups a rare opportunity to push their agenda more forcefully in the national arena.

The Székely Land CONIFA team, then, are an extension of a well-established and distinct historical region. While the team themselves play down their separatist ambitions, their supporters are less subtle in their approach, and the Hungarian nationalists that most commonly back their calls from the other side of the Romanian border are rarely of the same compromising disposition.

Those cultural roots run heavily through the team. The Székelys are captained by Csaba Csizmadia, a former Hungarian international who was born in the capital of the old Magyar Autonomous Region, Târgu Mureş. The rest of the squad is made up largely of players from Romanian third division team FK Miercurea Ciuc, a side from the region appropriately nicknamed 'The Szeklers'. Key forward István Fülöp is a member of that team that were abused at Dinamo, Sepsi OSK, a club now fairly well established in the top tier of the

Romanian league. Coach Robert Ilyes is a former Rapid Bucharest player who also hails from the region. In short, both the cultural links and the quality available to an 'unofficial' team is very solid.

The Hungarians' opponents on matchday two are the Zimbabweans, Matabeleland, who have drawn some extra attention due to an unlikely possible player call-up. The team have been making noises about formally calling up Bruce Grobbelaar, present around the side as a goalkeeping coach, into their squad, and putting the 60-year-old back between the sticks. Ultimately, Grobbelaar doesn't appear on the day, but does turn out later in the tournament.

When things get underway in front of what quickly becomes a wall of flairs and passionate chanting, the Székelys have a substantial level of control. Matabeleland do start strongly, however, creating a number of pacey and threatening moves down the wings. Had they been able to find the critical touch in the opening few minutes, things may have been very different.

Instead, the balance of the game turns entirely on a 23rd minute red card, given to Matabeleland's goalkeeper (and highest level professional) Thandazani Mdlongwa. Mdlongwa isn't setting a great example: he charges out of his area to try and cut out an incisive through ball, rashly taking out an advancing Székely striker in the process, though not before a looping shot is sent just wide of the mark.

From then on, Matabeleland are under near constant pressure. A similar through ball to the red card incident leads to a penalty, which is tucked away by Fülöp. Young FK Miercurea Ciuc men Arthur Gyorgyi and Szilárd Magyari add two more before half time, the first, from Gyorgyi, a beautifully placed freekick from distance. Two more goals in a 5-0 win each expose more than a little naivety in Matabeleland's defensive frailties. Székely Land, having played two relatively weak sides, still feel untested, though their hordes of fiery, beery followers celebrate wildly regardless.

The win confirms Székely Land's progression to the quarter finals with a game to spare, and eliminates Matabeleland from the sharp end of the competition. Regardless, the Zimbabweans in

Haringey Borough's small selection of seats are on their feet, dancing and singing their team off the field as they strain to be heard over the passionate Hungarians.

This unlikely match up of mid-level pros and passionate amateurs personifies CONIFA: it's a little one-sided, but nevertheless frantically paced and slightly feverish, enthusiastically backed and loaded with meaning for those on the pitch. The game has a passion in its challenges and engaged involvement from the players that's rare to see. It's easily the best 5-0 thrashing I've ever seen.

*

For me, writing about CONIFA took quite some planning. There's a bit of leap of faith involved in scheduling a summer holiday's worth of time off around the kind of competition that - from outside of those with a vested interest - is seen as a footballing curiosity. The launch into the unknown was proving colourful, but I'd decided I needed the occasional change of scene, too, even if it didn't involve anything all that different.

I'd long nominated that first Saturday of the tournament as the one day I was going to allow myself a slight deviation from ten days of wall-to-wall CONIFA. Oddly, my planned change of scene looped back to CONIFA's event. In an extended interview with General Secretary of CONIFA Sascha Düerkop ahead of the tournament, one of the things that had leapt out at me was the wildly diverse selection of grounds the organisation had explored as possible host venues.

Düerkop admitted that CONIFA had needed to contact virtually every club in London, down to the 9th tier of English football, in an attempt to put the tournament together. Starting at Arsenal and Chelsea, they kept going down as far as was necessary to find matchday venues.

Some had been ruled out as the clubs weren't interested. Many more were eliminated by the need to re-lay or rest grass pitches

53

between professional seasons, part of the reason that of all the grounds used by CONIFA in London, only Enfield Town's Hayes Lane ground wasn't home to a 3G pitch. The final choices, essentially, weren't so much the product of careful deliberation, as the ones that a process of elimination left standing.

At that time, I first spoke to Düerkop, three months ahead of the tournament, England's 90,000 capacity home Wembley Stadium - the second largest stadium in Europe - was still a serious contender to host the finale. "We're optimistic, and talks are ongoing," Düerkop had told me. He also dropped in a number of other major clubs, including Charlton and Millwall, who had seriously considered hosting the finale, but were ultimately hampered by pitch laying concerns ahead of the new season. None of those talks came to fruition, but they did highlight the ambitions CONIFA carried into the London event.

I decided to use my imagination, and check out what could have been at Wembley. Instead of staying for the second game in Haringey, I'd decided to head to England's pre-World Cup friendly against Nigeria under the arch, a game that was unusually underhyped. In contrast to the usual buzz overdrive, the England side were being played down in the media ahead of the World Cup in Russia, a factor that many believe may have played into their eventual, (and rare, overachieving) fourth place finish.

As you might have guessed from the topic of this book, grassroots football is far more my thing than top-level internationals. The games I most often attend are in a regional Irish third tier, the Leinster Senior League. Having said that, I am a lifelong Aston Villa fan (and former season ticket holder) - insert joke about the Birmingham club playing at that level soon enough here - and being Dublin based, have made a habit of dropping in on Ireland internationals when the tickets are reasonably priced.

I had been to the old Wembley, once, as a schoolboy to watch an underage game between England and Brazil. The old Wembley was tumbledown but monolithic, something a ten-year-old never forgets. Still, I'd never been to a full England international, despite being, by birth, and varying levels of passion, an England fan.

Strolling up Wembley Way, I was immediately glad the CONIFA finals weren't to be hosted at Wembley. While I can imagine what a celebration it would be for relatively low-level players to appear on a stage like this, I found the new stadium to be cold and uninspiring, the feel of the venue very much 'corporate day out'. The best moments of my visit came courtesy of the away fans.

I spent the long journey from Wood Green station near Haringey to Wembley chatting to Nigeria fans, who were buzzing with excitement about every aspect of their team. "Bring back Obafemi Martins, he's still only 18" rang through the green-packed subway carriages, in reference to their former star man, whose true age has often been in dispute.

More quietly, mothers in colourful patterned dresses complained that the team's extremely popular new World Cup shirt was completely sold out everywhere, and that they had no idea how to get one ahead of Russia 2018 getting underway. Later, in Wembley Way's tunnel, dozens of Nigerian fans formed an excited mini mosh pit as they leapt about singing the praises of unheralded Arsenal forward Alex Iwobi. Their team, and fans, were very much a celebration of what it is to be a Nigerian, and it was infectious.

As soon as I stepped inside the Wembley, though, I found the atmosphere flat and indifferent, with none of the chatty warmth and enthralled politics that came as a natural aside at the alternative World Cup. I have no doubt it's different at major tournaments, but England fans' support felt conditional and timid, in stark contrast to the vocal Matabeleland and Szekely Land fans I'd left behind, passionately lighting up CONIFA's side line. England won 2-1, but to me, it felt a little like watching on TV, minus the close ups: engaging at times, yes, but not particularly involved.

I'd missed seven games at CONIFA on one afternoon, but that's how the tournament's compression works. That wasn't as bad as it sounds: I'd made one game, and in practise it wasn't possible to see more than two, due to location and time clashes. Here's what went on around the grounds while I watched England hint at what was to follow in Russia...

*

Following Saturday's games, Group A was all set up to be the very tightest of three-way battles on the final group stage Sunday, which CONIFA's compressed format placed only three days after the tournament got underway. On matchday two, Cascadia saw off hosts Barawa, putting both on three points, while Ellan Vannin went clear at the top with two wins from two, defeating the uninspiring and lacklustre Tamils.

Ellan Vannin's win in Carshalton saw the Isle of Man side totally dominate, but struggle to bother the scoreboard for long periods. They finally found the net early in the second half through Ste Whiteley, who managed to turn a sleepy-looking Tamil defence around and finish from ten yards, though not without Sundaralingam in the Tamil goal getting a touch. The 'keeper was proving Tamil Eelam's best player, and had earlier instinctively stopped an effort from point blank range to take things into the break at 0-0.

The Tamils hit the post and had a shot cleared off the line shortly after going behind, before Sam Caine put Ellan Vannin totally in control with a goal on the hour mark. The Manx side probably should have added more. While the result didn't formally eliminate the Tamils, who could still get to a potentially decisive three points, it made them rank outsiders to progress.

At the same venue, an increasingly impressive looking Cascadia side got the better of hosts Barawa with a strong physical display. Mohamed Bettamer headed the Somali diaspora side in front early on, nodding in a cross at the back post after a pacey move had evaded the physically intimidating Cascadia defence.

The North Americans came back strong, and had two goalmouth scrambles amount to nothing in a dominant period, before Josh Doughty turned in a cross from close range to equalise. Hector Morales put them in front right before halftime, tapping in a corner.

Barawa rallied a little, but the big, technical North Americans could have won by more, and the result had opened up their tournament.

In group B, widely seen as the tournament's strongest group, holders Abkhazia faced their first major challenge against late call-up Karpatalya, and didn't impress. The crunch match in Enfield saw Zsolt Gajdos hit a deflected goal inside ten minutes for the Hungarian/ Ukrainian side. Vocally-backed Abkhazia had several chances to come back into the game in a tight match up, including a close-range header turned away by the commanding Sepsi OSK man Béla Fejér in the Karpatalya goal.

Abkhazia ramped up the pressure and looked like they might scrape their way out of things. Instead, a sting in the tail came when István Sándor hit a long-range effort into the Abkhazia net eight minutes into second half injury time. With the Carpathian side scheduled to play fascinating (but relatively weak) Tibet in the final group game, they suddenly looked extremely likely to qualify. That left the group's big guns, Northern Cyprus and Abkhazia in big trouble, and set to play what was effectively an early knockout game that would end one team's hopes of bringing home the bacon.

The Tibet v Northern Cyprus game, also in Enfield, remained the best attended of the competition right up until the final. Enfield was picked as a venue for Northern Cyprus games due to its vast Turkish and Northern Cypriot community, many of whom turned out, draped in the red and white of their outcast nation. Tibet have their own unique following at the tournament, fascinated by the team's Buddhist routes, passive philosophy, and isolated footballing style. Over 2000 crammed the barriers in Enfield to watch a game almost certain to end one way.

The underdogs competed well. They slipped up defensively to allow Halil Turan to beat the offside trap near the halfway line and drill Northern Cyprus in front from range, but Tibet hit an unlikely and wildly-celebrated equaliser with a close range, slide-in goal from Kalsang Topgyal towards the end of the first half. The quest to hang on began.

Somewhat inevitably, the Northern Cypriots then took charge. Turan grabbed another from a tight angle with 25 minutes remaining, and Uğur Gök finished the game as a contest with a 73rd minute lob into the tiring Tibetans' net. The loss formally eliminated the traveling Asian side from the tournament, but with no little pride in their performances along the way.

Haringey Borough proved to be home of the thrashing of the day, a second 8-0 of the tournament. After Szekely Land earlier dismissed ten-man Matabeleland 5-0, struggling Tuvalu - the only indisputably recognised nation at the tournament - were thumped by ruthless North Italian group leaders Padania.

Federico Corno hit a hat trick before half time, with Giulio Valente adding three, two in the first half, as Padania ran rampant and went in 6-0 up at the break. Corno's second, scored off an intricate passing move, and a sharp second-half volley on the turn by William Rosset were the highlights, though the fans in Haringey preferred the underdog, and every Tuvalu attack was cheered to the rafters. The two results eliminated Tuvalu and Matabeleland, and left Padania and Szekely Land playing for position in their final Group C game.

Group D was far less of a goal fest, with United Koreans In Japan and Kabylia playing out a really poor quality 0-0 draw at Bracknell Town, before Western Armenia notched the only Group D goal of the day against Panjab in Slough. The impressive Vahagn Militosyan, who plays for Slovak top-tier side FC Nitra, was the scorer in a frantic and tetchy contest that could have gone either way and clearly left a bad taste in Panjab mouths. Militosyan's goal put Western Armenia top of the most open of groups, with every team still in with a chance of progressing.

Day two results (June 2, 2018):

Group A:
Tamil Eelam 0 - 2 Ellan Vannin
Barawa 1 - 2 Cascadia

Group B:
Karaptalya 2 - 0 Abkhazia
Northern Cyprus 3 - 1 Tibet (Tibet eliminated)

Group C:
Szekely Land 5 - 0 Matabeleland (Matabeleland eliminated)
Tuvalu 0 - 8 Padania (Tuvalu eliminated)

Group D:
Kabylia 0 - 0 United Koreans In Japan
Panjab 0 - 1 Western Armenia

The CONIFA Difference: How CONIFA's Tournaments Differ From Footballing Convention

FIFA's 2018 World Cup Final, France vs Croatia, had global viewing figures that were as near as makes no difference a billion people. With at least one - and arguably two - relatively unexpected finalists, and with much of the western world declaring Russia an inhospitable place full of hooligans, heavy-handed policing and other travel risks, the headline sponsors nevertheless included some of the biggest commercial outlets in the world, from McDonalds to Hyundai, Adidas to Visa. After all, how often can you reach a billion potential customers all at once?

CONIFA's London tournament also had its fair share of controversies, mostly around the teams taking part and their backgrounds. In terms of sponsorship, the result was somewhat different: if not for the involvement of carefree and quirk-loving Irish betting company Paddy Power, CONIFA 2018 might not have happened at all.

There are plenty of things that are, by necessity, different about CONIFA and its struggling organisation. It's almost intrinsic in what they do, and the circumstances they face. Unlike most national teams, many of the sides that turn out in London face political issues that make their appearance at the competition problematic before the team even makes it off the training ground.

The government they live under might object to their existence; they might be geographically isolated, or they might be forced to use players drawn from a global diaspora, due to issues with representation locally.

The first consequence of these problems is qualification has to be a little convoluted. There are no big groups of round-robin mini-leagues, certainly not in front of massive crowds. Only the more fortunate of the representative teams have any realistic chance of facing each other outside of a focused competition. The costs for the member entities would be too substantial, and the political fallout of drawing attention to themselves could also be difficult for some teams. Nevertheless, almost fifty CONIFA members must be narrowed down to the 16 that kick off in London somehow, and so CONIFA invent a qualification compromise.

In the bigger regions - Europe, Africa and Asia - teams have a set period of time to play a maximum of ten competitive games that count towards qualification. The premise is that the teams can each find some kind of opposition locally, whether it's a pub team, a university academy or, in some rare cases, semi-professional or fully professional opposition (Panjab played the Liverpool under-23 side and England C in the build up to the tournament, for example).

Even this concept isn't entirely effective: plenty of CONIFA teams opt not to even try and qualify each time around, for various reasons. Transnistria, Franconia, Heligoland, Monaco, Nagorno-Karabakh (Artsakh), Sápmi and Skaneland were all registered as European CONIFA teams ahead of 2018, and didn't play a single qualifying game for the 2018 tournament between them. Some teams, like Transnistria, are simply stuck in too volatile an environment to try and organise, while others, like the Rohingya side that opted out of Asian qualification, have domestic issues so substantial it's understandable football's a long way from the agenda (close to three million Rohingya Muslims have been forced into refugee status this decade, and thousands killed).

For those who do enter qualification, the process is laid out clearly in advance. Its flaws are obvious, but given the constraints on teams, coming up with a better way of narrowing things down isn't easy.

Each team gains a number of qualifying points awarded as a result of each game they're able to play, up to a maximum of nine points per game. These points are awarded according to two factors, and then summed for a total qualifying score, gained over no more than ten scoring qualifying games.

For each game, three 'results' points are awarded for a win, two for a draw and one for a loss. So far, so simple. This 'result' score is then multiplied by a 'value' assigned to the opposition. The valuation of opposition is somewhat simplistic and doesn't necessarily reflect an opponent's quality. It is designed to encourage competition between CONIFA members, and has the benefit of clarity.

The 'value' score is in effect a multiplier for the result: three points for a CONIFA member, two for another international side, and one point for any other opposition. 'Another national side is defined by CONIFA qualifying rules and to date, these have included sides like Jersey (who joined CONIFA shortly after the London tournament), Carinthian Slovenes, a UN Select XI and an Isle of Man side distinct from the Ellan Vannin one that plays within CONIFA. The process can be impressively confusing.

The total score for each game, then, is the assigned value of the team multiplied by the points score gained from the result. A win against another CONIFA side would result in a maximum nine qualification points (three points for the win x three points as a multiplier for the opposition beaten). You could call it a thought-out flaw that a loss against a CONIFA team would be worth three points (three points for the opposition x one for the loss), the same as a win against to any other local, non-national level opposition.

As an example, here is the qualifications series that helped Ellan Vannin into CONIFA's 2018 tournament:

Lost 0-3 v South Tyrol (result 1, opposition value 2) = 2 points
Lost 2-3 v North Frisians (result 1, opposition value 2) = 2 points
Won 2-0 v Germans in Upper Silesia (result 3, opposition value 2) = 6 points
Won 7-0 v Stockport Town FC XI (result 3, opposition value 1) = 3 points
Lost 0-1 v Padania (result 1, opposition value 3) = 3 points
Won 1-0 v Fevidek (result 3, opposition value 3) = 9 points
Lost 2-4 v Szekely Land (result 1, opposition value 3) = 3 points
Drew 3-3 v Karapatalya (result 2, opposition value 3) = 6 points

Won 6-2 v Barawa (result 3, opposition value 3) = 9 points
Won 12-0 v Chagos Islands (result 3, opposition value 3) = 9 points

TOTAL = 52 points.

Ellan Vannin's total of 52 points put them top of European qualifying, a comfortable qualifying score, but they certainly benefited from playing an abundance of other CONIFA sides, six in total.

There's no question a system set up like this could benefit a group of teams that are able to play each other on a regular basis, or perhaps the well-funded or less politically volatile sides that have the option to travel. Under the circumstances, though, it's hard to envisage a qualifying criterion that would be entirely, indisputably fair.

The tallies across up to ten games are the key criteria that teams have to consider. They make up the absolute maximum score of 90 points for qualification - with the top scoring teams for each region admitted to the tournament. The number of places allocated to each continent is worked out by dividing the number of CONIFA entities from that region by the total number of entities globally, and then multiplying by the number of qualifying places available for the tournament. A little rounding along the way favours the little guys. This is CONIFA, after all.

To give a few other examples, in Asian qualifying, Panjab's 2-0 win against Jersey was critical to their qualification, with Jersey's 'quality of opposition' value assigned at two (a national, non-CONIFA member), meaning Panjab scored six of their 18 qualifying points from just that one game.

The win lifted Panjab above Iraqi Kurdistan, who played seven games and won five of them (they drew one and lost one of the other two), as all Kurdistan's opposition were neither CONIFA nor international sides. The last VIVA World Cup winners gained 15 points, and sat three short of the qualification mark, and so didn't meet the criteria to travel to London. That seems a little harsh on

Kurdistan, with Panjab able to play CONIFA opposition far more locally, but such is life.

Qualification in Europe was the most competitive, with Ellan Vannin's winning tally of 52 qualifying points taken largely from a host of other CONIFA teams, as shown above. These results also meant Ellan Vannin were unusually familiar with their CONIFA opponents coming into the tournament, while teams like Matabeleland and Tuvalu arrived having never played any of the opponents they would face.

Ellan Vannin qualified alongside Szekely Land, who'd played seven unbeaten qualifying games against largely top-end CONIFA opposition. The pair were joined, ultimately, by late replacements Karpatalya, who had just missed out on third place before Felvidek, another Hungarian region side, withdrew in the last couple of months ahead of the tournament.

Two other sides just missed out in Europe. Greenland played eleven games in their attempt to qualify, but did not win many of them, and had the final one automatically disallowed, due to the ten-game maximum. Occitania (a region in the south of France) played eight, and would likely have qualified had they played a ninth. Six teams had played games in attempting to qualify, but not made it, while another eight hadn't kicked a ball in trying to get to London.

The qualifying system is well understood by the teams involved, but also somewhat convoluted, in particular around teams assigned 'quality' scores. The scores have the benefit of not being subjective, but would definitely disadvantage a team playing strong, non-CONIFA opposition (they'd be better of being cynical and playing a local pub team if they can't find someone with a higher points value, and at least ensuring they consistently win), and a team unable to find CONIFA opposition locally. Given the criteria are agreed by the teams taking part, they don't have much cause for complaint.

That's the bulk of the qualifying set up, but it's not quite all.

The 'play your way in' method of qualifying for CONIFA tournaments is not quite the FIFA World Cup's groups, playoffs and international rivalries, but it's certainly not easy, and the executive recognise it favours teams who face favourable circumstances. Because it's so difficult for some teams to conceivably qualify for the tournament, there is an alternative. Two teams in London were 'voted' into the tournament as Wild Cards.

The South Pacific island of Kiribati were simply handed their place by a vote of all CONIFA members at the organisation's annual general meeting in January 2018. The place was awarded in part in recognition of the qualification issues that come about as a result of their isolation, and the sheer cost of either bringing opposition to the island, or traveling to play opponents.

The other criteria that appealed to the members was the need for Kiribati - in this case through their football side - to represent its substantial issues around climate change. The highest point in Kiribati is 81 metres above sea level, but the average height of the collection of atolls and coral islands is just 2.5 metres above sea level. Consistent sea level rises threaten to completely overwhelm most of the low-lying islands - which are spread across a vast 3.5 million sq kms of ocean - in the coming years.

Ultimately, Kiribati didn't get to present their cause or flaunt their skills for the most mundane of reasons: money. Flights out of Kiribati are notoriously pricey. Their even smaller and equally isolated 'neighbours' Tuvalu did manage to gather funds together, and took their place, as the only other representative from the region.

Tuvalu is 1,600kms away from Kiribati, but neighbourly by South Pacific standards, a stat that demonstrates the qualification difficulties faced by the two countries. This isolation has had broader sporting effects, too. The pair are widely accepted as legitimate countries and UN members, but, despite years of lobbying by Kiribati in particular, have never been accepted into more conventional international football by FIFA. Tibet - a popular member of CONIFA who bring a unique sporting brand - were voted in as the other Wild Card side.

There are other 'gifts' into the tournament, too. Tournament hosts Barawa were given a 'free in' as hosts, as happens in most international football tournaments. Cascadia were technically required to qualify, but the only other North American side at the time of the qualification, Quebec, hadn't yet formally joined CONIFA when qualification took place. As a result, the west coast men effectively got a bye, and played their first ever international game in London, on the opening day of the tournament.

If the whole process seems odd, it's worth keeping in mind that most reasonable alternatives would instantly exclude some of the smaller and more isolated entities, or, to put it another way, go entirely against the premise of the organisation itself. It's hard to envisage a scenario that would be both completely fair, and cater to CONIFA's remit in connecting with its inaccessible and commonly disregarded fringes.

The result is certainly imbalance, but that is, it seems, an intended consequence. There's no question that some of the teams arrived in London with no reasonable chance of progressing beyond the group stage. Teams like Tuvalu and Tibet play isolated, largely untested football and have no players of any real repute. When they come up against the likes of Padania, or Northern Cyprus, they're simply out of their depth, in terms of experience, resources, match fitness, or most other reasonable criteria you might be able to think of. Of course, they'd like to do more, but the key victory for teams like Tibet, Tuvalu and Matabeleland, it seems, comes through representation itself.

On the flipside, the qualification process does seem to give access to the very strongest teams, and ensure that the summit of CONIFA's tournaments is full of as much talent as can be mustered. The strength runs from traditional powerhouses of non-FIFA football in Padania and Abkhazia, to fast-rising CONIFA world number one Panjab as well as the two fiercely competitive Hungarian-linked teams, Szekely Land and Karpatalya. It's hard to say if the best CONIFA-affiliated sides all appeared in London without a point of comparison, but the better teams were genuinely technically impressive, and seemed to have the potential to compete at a fairly decent club level.

While qualification is complex, politics also plays into the organisation, even while it tries to avoid any political impact at all. Tibet's involvement in London, for example, had a particularly large effect, after CONIFA came under pressure from sponsors to remove the side. As they had been with other sides in the past, CONIFA were steadfast in their refusal to even consider throwing the Tibetan side out even under substantial pressure.

The Tibetan squad is not based in Tibet, but made up of Tibetans based largely in the Dalai Lama's exile town of Dharamshala, as the Chinese government simply would not consider letting a Tibetan representative side out of Chinese-occupied Tibet to compete. As a result, the Tibetan side was actually a Tibetan diaspora side, if one largely drawn from a small area of India now steeped in Tibetan history. Nevertheless, they still drew substantial Chinese consternation.

While the side came with a personal blessing from the Dalai Lama, they were something of a curse for the organisers, through no fault of their own. CONIFA Director Paul Watson revealed to The Independent that several six-figure sponsorships had been lined up to contribute to the London tournament a few months ahead of kick off. Each had then asked, one by one, for Tibet to be kicked out. On CONIFA's refusal, each company then withdrew their proposed sponsorship, leaving a serious, existential strain on the tournament.

It's assumed the Chinese government are behind the pressure, which, fortunately, ultimate title sponsor Paddy Power chose to ignore. "People are scared to sponsor an event like this because they're afraid of offending China, a big market for many of them" Watson had said. That Tibet did play is a sign of CONIFA's strength against the pressures of external politics. With Tibet given a wild card in the first place, this entire, largely predictable problem could have been avoided earlier in the process if CONIFA had wanted to go down a less bumpy road, but they opted to stick firmly to their beliefs.

"These teams applied because they were either insufficiently active or did not have the qualification results to qualify for the tournament on a results basis alone," Sacha Duerkop, general secretary said of the wild card process. "Tibet's application was compelling and the executive committee granted the wild card on that basis." The pressure that followed never seemed to be a consideration, at least publicly.

The Chinese weren't the only government making bold moves behind the scenes. Cascadia-backing American website Prost Amerika learnt ahead of the tournament of a letter writing campaign by the Cypriot government's London representatives, which saw pressure asserted on the already depleted range of host stadiums, and the clubs that run them, to withdraw their support from the competition. The Cypriot government's issue was with the involvement of Northern Cyprus, a state that exists behind a UN-enforced buffer zone running right through island capital Nicosia, and still bitterly opposed on the southern half of the island. Only Turkey formally recognises Northern Cyprus.

Prost Amerika's research included uncovering a letter given to them anonymously by one of the host clubs, who had received it from the Cypriot Deputy High Commissioner in London, Solon Savva. In it, Savva writes:

"I would like to kindly request that [club name redacted by Prost] urgently reconsider its decision to allow the use of the stadium for the so-called CONIFA Paddy Power World Football Cup 2018, and possibly for matches of the so-called 'Northern Cyprus' football team."

The letters are dated late enough that the club's withdrawal of facilities would have presented a serious problem for the organisers. They go on to attack CONIFA itself, stating:

"Irrespective of what CONIFA likes to call itself, this is an association that provides an umbrella network for illegal secessionist entities purportedly to play football. Regrettably, under the guise of football, some of the CONIFA members use the association and its tournaments as a means to further their political agendas and goals."

"One of the members of CONIFA is the so-called 'Turkish Republic of Northern Cyprus (TRNC)', or 'Northern Cyprus', which is nothing more than an illegal secessionist entity created in the northern occupied part of Cyprus by Turkey through the use of force in 1974."

As well as Cypriot representatives, the Acting Deputy High Commissioner for Sri Lanka got involved, with the Tamil Eelam side his target. Sugeeshwara Gunaratna made no attempt to actually stop the Tamil's playing in London, but he did throw out a press release regardless.

"I wish to bring to your attention that a territory entitled 'Tamil Eelam' does not exist, nor has it existed in Sri Lanka either de facto or de jure," he said

"It may be noted that the Liberation Tigers of Tamil Eelam (LTTE), a terrorist organisation proscribed in a number of countries including Sri Lanka, India, USA, Europe and Canada, carried out a violent campaign in Sri Lanka in order to create a country by this name. However, their violent campaign of death and destruction was brought to an end in May 2009."

We'll deal with the specifics of CONIFA's politics - or, in almost all cases, its attempt to avoid politics - later in this book, but for now it suffices to say the above opinions are more than a little one-sided in their outlook, and, looked at objectively, somewhat overrate the impact of a football team on establishing a region's legitimacy, or otherwise.

Looking past the politics - which is often weighty enough to be a difficult aspect to ignore - there are plenty of small changes made for CONIFA tournaments that play into the spirit and identity of the organisation, especially when it comes to what goes on actually on the pitch. Tournaments are compressed into a dense flood of matches, for example, with each team playing six games in just nine days. This isn't ideal from a sporting perspective, but things are held this way to make travel as affordable as possible for teams from poor and isolated regions of the globe.

By only having to stay in London for ten days, the tournament becomes that bit more affordable than a conventional FIFA or UEFA Championship could ever be. Most of the teams shack up together in large, shared accommodation, sharing training facilities, a fleet of buses and bulk-ordered meals. Tournaments of the same number of games at UEFA European Championship level are typically played over around 24 days, and only the final two (or in some years, four) teams will play a full six games. Until recently, a full half of the sides were dispatched home after three.

CONIFA's Knockout games go directly to penalties for a similar reason. It's hard to imagine even the fully-loaded squads of 23 players (the same size as nations bring to FIFA tournaments) competing effectively across six games in nine days, and then finding the energy to go into additional time as well.

Naturally, there is far more squad rotation than you'd expect at the FIFA World Cup. In fact, for some of the locally-based teams, availability drops off substantially below 23 players anyway for midweek games, for mundane reasons as simple as having to go to work, or spend time with family.

There are changes to the very core of the game, too, ones that reach into the heart of what modern football has become, and try to tweak it. One of the aims of CONIFA is to foster fair play. That's particularly important in trying to develop a good relationship between teams which might be politically opposed, as a positive relationship between such entities is essential to the organisation's future viability. CONIFA couldn't exist with credibility should it become easy to demonstrate that they favour one political position heavily over another.

One of the innovations used to encourage fairness is the 'green card', introduced for the first time in London. The green card is for offences deemed 'between' a red and yellow card. The idea is borrowed from the Irish Gaelic Athletics Association (GAA), where the concept is also relatively new.

The GAA uses a black card, instead of green, but the basic principle is similar. Players who commit certain types of fouls - at CONIFA, these are dissent towards anyone from officials to the crowd, and diving - are sent from the field of play, but can be replaced by another player in a forced substitution. The offending side might be disadvantaged by the enforced substitution of a first-choice player, but can still play on without a numerical disadvantage.

"If a particular player behaves badly on the pitch, the green card gives the referee the opportunity to sanction him personally without sanctioning the whole team, as they will be able to continue with the full 11 players," General Secretary Sascha Duerkop said of the concept.

"Sportsmanship and fair play are absolute core values and we spent years discussing how we could eradicate the typical bad behaviours on a football pitch seen in nearly every match today - simulating, arguing, shouting names - more effectively than others have done."

The introduction has been broadly positive in GAA, and has seemingly reduced the amount of professional fouling in killing off games, something that was previously rife. Players, obviously, don't want to be dismissed from the field. The main criticism has been that the rule further disadvantages weaker squads.

A strong side with a depth of quality on the bench might be able to replace a player with another of similarly ability, while a weak squad is likely to be lacking a player of comparable ability in every position. That might alter the dynamic of the game slightly, but if it cuts out diving and full-on refereeing protests, for example, it's easy to see how a lot of football fans might get behind it.

The final key change in the way CONIFA sets up is the absence of the tradition of being 'knocked out' of a cup tournament. Instead, teams compete for every position, from one to 16. As the tournament progresses, the irregularity of matches outside of tournaments means every game takes on some significance, as the sides find their place in CONIFA's equivalent of the FIFA world rankings. No game is truly meaningless, especially when you're taking a rare chance to represent your identity.

Panjab were ranked CONIFA number one going into the London tournament, a status they were extremely proud of, and while rankings were only a guideline, the accuracy of that status was unquestionably improved by each team playing six times when they are together.

With all the sides in the same place for ten days - a real rarity - tournaments finish with everyone playing their way through into their own level. If you come in third or fourth in your group, you find yourself playing 'knockout' games to place somewhere between 9th and 16th towards the end of the tournament. Win on any day after the group games, and your final rank will be higher than that of your opponents. Lose and you'll place lower. There tend to be a lot of penalties.

On the final day, there isn't only a fiercely contested final and a third/ fourth place play off, but also a battle for seventh and eighth, and a battle for fifteenth and sixteenth, almost as fiercely contested by teams looking for their first ever international win, or looking at seeding for next time around. Then, every side gathers in Hayes Lane, Enfield for the finale and the closing ceremony. Ultimately, with every side having played six games, their status is narrowed down to a single place, from 1st to 16th.

Soon, they hope, CONIFA will be expanding their footballing reach a little further, though it's not clear quite when just yet. For future tournaments, as well as the rule changes, CONIFA is also looking into introducing some new versions of the game to their repertoire. That's likely to start with the introduction of a lady's tournament, a futsal tournament, and football for the disabled. Always ambitious, CONIFA also have age-group contests on the agenda for the future.

Matabeleland: Football on a Wing and a Prayer

Founded: 2016 *Record Win:* 3-1 v Tuvalu *Record Loss:* 6-1 v Padania *Distance Travelled to London:* 5253 miles (8453 kms) *Home Capital:* Bulawayo, Zimbabwe *Player Pool Playing In:* Zimbabwe *CONIFA Ranking:* unranked

It's a month before the 2018 CONIFA World Football Cup, and Englishman Justin Walley is sat in front of his computer completing his latest bout of unlikely admin on behalf of a team of amateur Zimbabwean footballers. Walley signed on as a football manager, but has become something far more: part social media manager, part financial boss, part skills coach and a man required to hop through countries and across continents in an attempt to train the inexperienced, and fund the seemingly impossible.

The man from Leicestershire, now resident in Riga, Latvia, is an unlikely frontman for Bulawayo-based Matabeleland's campaign to reach London. Having got involved in CONIFA after one of their executive members contacted him looking to add some Latvian club jerseys to his extensive shirt collection, Walley found a group of likeminded, ambitious football fans, and quickly made friends. Eventually, he connected more firmly with the organisation, too, and become its African Director.

With four weeks to go until London, Walley finds himself desperately trying to sell Matabeleland's stunningly designed kits in order to fund flights, visas and accommodation for his players. On top of the shirts - two beautifully unusual, tribally-patterned collector's items - his crowdfunding campaign also includes meals with the players in London, the option to train with the team, and corporate sponsorship opportunities. For the less flush, there are spots as a mascot at each of the team's games, Matabeleland pendants, and even pieces of Zimbabwe's inflation-hit currency up for sale. The fundraising target is a hefty $40,000.

This is not, it's fair to say, how journeys to international football tournaments typically start. Matabeleland's last-gasp securing of visas and the funds necessary to travel to London is tight - too tight for the comfort of Walley and his squad - but also poignant and heart-warming. Walley's borderline begging on behalf of his squad on social media simply reflects his passion for what this side have achieved. Ultimately, it's a loan from the manager's mother, paid back after the tournament, that pushes the team's funding over the line and gets them on the plane.

Walley's side are not the first from the region to face substantial barriers to qualifying in recent times. To say the Zimbabwe national team's campaign to qualify for the 2018 FIFA World Cup in Russia was a disaster is something of an understatement. The Warriors have never made an intercontinental competition, and they weren't expected to this time, either, with the side's best days a couple of decades in the past. Somehow, they undershot even their own fans low expectations, as the only African nation not to even kick off the qualifying tournament for Russia.

The failure to compete came after Zimbabwe were expelled from FIFA qualifying as early as March 2015, punished for refusing to pay a former coach his contractual severance fee. That decision made The Warriors one of the first teams to be officially eliminated from the 2018 World Cup, more than three years and three months before kick-off.

Like other CONIFA teams, this Matabeleland squad doesn't have a single player involved with that national team, or even particularly close to it. Most of the Zimbabwean internationals play abroad, at clubs ranging from Leicester City to Sweden's Djurgården and Egypt's El-Entag El-Harby. Those who don't ply their trade elsewhere certainly play at the absolute peak of Zimbabwe's homegrown Castle Lager Soccer League, playing ball with clubs like Champions FC Platinum, and the wonderfully named upper mid-table sides Chicken Inn and How Mine.

Both of those two mid-table, colourfully-monikered clubs are based in Matabeleland provincial capital Bulawayo, in fact, but the Matabeleland squad is a little different, and substantially more amateur than even the Zimbabwean top-tier. When Bruce Grobbelaar describes the squad he comes to be part of, he suggests some of the players almost literally come from a background that amounts to little more than playing in the streets.

Infrastructure is unquestionably a problem. Since 2006, the Matabele region has had a separatist party campaigning for independence from a position of exile in South Africa. The Matabeleland Freedom Party call vocally for an independent country under a constitutional monarchy.

Their separatist reasoning makes for a strong case. The region was targeted by Robert Mugabe during his long reign in Zimbabwe, largely because the Ndebele people are of a different tribal origin to Mugabe's Shona people, and tended to malign Mugabe.

Over the course of decades, Matabeleland suffered an estimated 30,000 deaths at the hands of their own Mugabe-led government and his forces. In particular, the region was regularly targeted by a group called 5 Brigade, led by a brutal warlord, Perence 'Black Jesus' Shiri, so named as he could decide the course of a life, like Jesus.

Shiri's army were gruesome: their crimes included the raping of village women, and later returning to kill those who had become pregnant as a result of the rape. They buried alive those who they suspected even thought to oppose Mugabe, and forced other villagers to dance atop the graves of their neighbours, all while chanting songs in praise of Mugabe's government.

Later, the region was starved of supplies, with shops not allowed to restock shelves, and beatings dished out to those who chose to share limited food with their neighbours. Insult was added to substantial injury when 'Black Jesus' claimed a large amount of compensation from Mugabe's government's tax revenue for what were very likely falsified war injury claims, worked his way to the heart of a huge illicit diamond trade (all whilst siphoning off profit), and was then allowed to study at the Royal College of Defence

Studies in London. The region's substantially more positive other key claim to fame is as the birthplace of scouting, under Robert Baden Powell.

Busani Sibindi is the President of Matabeleland football, a role he takes on alongside his full-time work as an NGO head and activist with the Save Matabeleland Coalition, an organisation he founded in 2013. "These things are all interconnected," Sibindi tells me of the team and his other work. "The Save Matabeleland Coalition is the main organisation that houses these projects, things like the team. We also work with various affiliates to make things work."

"In Matabeleland we have got football and arts," he continues. "These are like second nature to us. Football is more than a hobby to us. Most of the guys who play football in this part of the country use it as a kind of empowerment. They also use it as a way of getting out of a lot of other problems that may be affecting them. But most people see it as an opportunity to go to other places and improve their lives."

"I founded the Matabeleland Football Team in 2016 and it has however grown tremendously over the last two years. The players come from different backgrounds. A few of them are playing in semi-professional and professional leagues, while some of them are straight from grassroots and amateurs. Some are students learning and some are professionals working."

"All of them have one thing in common: they love football and have been playing it since they were children. We do, however, have a significant number who are not doing anything except playing football, and we hope one day they will make it professionally. We also try to work with other partners who can provide employment for those who are coming of age and have no prospect of playing soccer professionally in the longer run."

Many of these players were scouted out by the project in the early days of the Matabeleland football, uncovered all over the province and invited to take part. Some are drawn from as far afield as seven to eight hours north of the team's home base of Bulawayo, and have relocated their lives to take part.

"You have to recognise that football is a very simple sport to start playing," Sibindi says of the local appeal of the game. "You only need a pitch and a ball most of the time. When we were growing up as young boys, we would make plastic balls from trash. You could use those without even going to buy one from the store, so we didn't need anything. If you've got challenges in life, soccer clubs give you some kind of social status."

"For the people of Matabeleland, this is a massive breakthrough. It's a peace building initiative that gives people hope. It gives people who have lost a lot of self-belief value in their own lives. When we go to London, we're going to play for all those things, and restore a lot of dignity for the people of Matabeleland."

"Most people are relieved and feel happy that there is some change happening in the country. Personally, I think change is a transition. We don't expect things to all of a sudden become perfect, but we think that there is hope, now that there has been a change," Busindi says of the departure of Mugabe and the progress being made in Matabeleland. "Change is good, even if it's transitioning from something that is good to something that is better."

Ahead of the tournament, social media pictures show the Matabeleland squad jogging down the side of dusty roads in matching t-shirts. Large lorries pass inches from them, but they're smiling as the sweat drips from their heat-pressured bodies. The opportunity they're being given is a rare one for people from such backgrounds, and every moment of it, no matter how tough, is to be savoured.

"They come from hard situations, difficult situations," Busani Khanye, a member of the Matabeleland football Confederacy, explains of the team. "We are now a family. With the guys, you are never just coaches and directors. We are brothers, uncles, care givers. They come and explain their problems to us. We can move along together, sharing problems together." That close-knit passion for the unlikely project really shines in London.

When the Matabeleland squad arrive at their first game in the city, they dance from their team bus into Sutton United's Gander

Lane, down the tunnel towards their changing rooms and into the rugged heart of the stand, chanting in their native Ndebele as they go. Half an hour later, they emerge onto the 3G pitch in a black kit littered with complex red and yellow patterns, several players reaching down to pick at and scratch at the fake grass beneath their feet.

It's been a long journey from this relatively rural, poor province in the west of Zimbabwe. While many of the African teams represented at CONIFA draw their squads mostly from their British diaspora, Matabeleland have exclusively been plucked from their own region, and developed as a team that's a pure, unfiltered representation of Matabeleland. With the exception of a couple of short trips to South Africa and a trip to Zambia as part of the qualifying process, almost no member of the playing staff has ever left his own country before now.

Manager Justin Walley is very much the opposite. Inspired by a trip to Riga during a year-long travel jaunt, Walley relocated to Latvia when his trip was over, citing the capital city's beauty, party atmosphere, and women as the main draw. A speedy winger in his day, football had long run through his life, with his Riga United side well-established, rising up the leagues to grab a bronze medal in the Latvia women's league. The team had been handed over to its members, and Walley stumbled quite by chance upon his new challenge.

Matabeleland's call for a coach seemed speculative, but Walley's international exploration meant his coaching experience with Riga United had led to only modest qualifications in the role, so he was excluded from bigger offers that might better reflect his extensive coaching experience. The English FA had turned down his requests to take part in their UEFA coaching courses as he was not willing to relocate back to England. Their Latvian counterparts were similarly uninspired, fearing he would leave, taking their investment with him. Walley had football management ambitions, though, and Matabeleland seemed the perfect fit.

Training sessions were to be an experience. The October before CONIFA's London tournament was to get underway, Walley first travelled to Bulawayo - a city he calls "a really run-down colonial town" - to meet a dedicated squad lacking some of the most basic facilities.

His men were training with two balls, one of which was quite flat. They had no bibs to identify teams, and no cones to complete basic exercises. Playing on a hardened pitch, they didn't have any real experience of football on grass, at least not as they could expect to encounter in Europe. On a visa run to neighbouring Botswana, Walley spent $100 on basic training equipment, and set about preparing his team.

The hardest part was always going to be money. A provincial squad with minor footballing connections from a poor rural corner of East Africa had no realistic chance of raising the cash to sort visas and accommodation for the ten days in London they required, so Walley set about that serious crowdfunding campaign, backing his side's ambition.

"The first time I saw them, they were playing a friendly against a Zimbabwean second tier team," he recalls. "They had a team, and had qualified by playing lots of fixtures against local clubs and a CONIFA side in Zambia. They were very good on fitness, but in certain senses, they weren't very good at all. Particularly upper body strength, stuff like that."

"Tactically the team was quite naive. My opinion was a lot of that needed to be changed around. I did all the technical stuff across a few sessions, then I was away for about two or three months. They kind of went with what I set up, and developed a new way of playing."

"When I got there, we had one training pitch, and it was summer, so it was very dry. It had next to no grass on it and was very uneven. It wasn't a shocking, shocking pitch by African standards, but it was rubbish. Some of the away pitches we played on, they had glass on, poo, stuff like that. Shocking, really. We didn't have money, so before long we started training on the public pitch, which was just a dirt patch, really."

"The pitches in London were a massive issue for us. We got new blades from Bruce Grobbelaar [who came on board in support of Matabeleland] and had one training session in them before the games started, so that was a struggle. The pitch, the bounce... they play so quickly back home, and the players started misjudging the bounce. Honestly, if we'd been able to play football on the surfaces we were used to, we'd have beaten a lot of teams. You can't play football on those surfaces without practise. I don't know how they do it, on those pitches. They know the pace of the bounce, which is very quick. It's very different, very strange."

"When I got there, there were two balls, a set of cones, and a couple of bibs. Doing a decent session was impossible. The shooting sessions, they'd be kicking the ball and then waiting for it to come back from behind the goal. We had no nets. Somebody spooned one and it's over into the gardens and everyone's stood around."

The entire set up in Matabeleland, then, would have been unacceptable to a park club in London. Unhygienic and sometimes dangerous pitches, combined with an almost complete absence of equipment or resources was to make the entire process a big uphill battle. Walley was determined to make it work.

The involvement of Bruce Grobbelaar in the side was a major coup for the Zimbabweans, both in terms of the motivation and status he provided. His appearances in London alongside the players became one of the tournament's talking points. "I just emailed him, and he replied three days later," Walley recalls. "We agreed to meet to have a chat. I met him at the M6 services in Wolverhampton, and just asked him to join us."

Getting a big-name former pro involved might seem like a no-brainer, but even Grobbelaar's very welcome inclusion wasn't without its concerns for Walley as he prepared to travel.

"I was thinking by him agreeing, he might end up in the shit somehow, and I'd feel responsible," Walley explained, acknowledging the political sensitivity of the situation. "He liked the project. Highlanders FC, from Bulawayo in Matabeleland was his first professional club, and he wanted to be involved. He liked the concept."

"I think for half an hour he was casing me out, whether I was genuine, and then I convinced him that what we were doing was worth getting involved in. He's been involved in lots of things in his life, including things like the Rhodesian Bush War. He's a very experienced man, and I think he can make judgements for himself on what's in his best interests. I think he enjoyed being involved, and he might well be involved again."

For Walley, though, expectations remained modest. Even if having secured a trip beyond their wildest dreams, his players were somewhat more optimistic about what their appearance in London might hold.

"We weren't coming to the tournament to win," the manager said. "I think some of the players might have thought we were, and I did try to explain that it's just not realistic. If we'd had another six months, though, it might have been different. We were about five players short, including a lad from Halifax Town, Cliff Moyo, when we went out. The Szekely Land President said that if we had played them in a year's time, he thinks we'd have beaten them."

There's no question the Matabeleland side has plenty going for them. Physically fit and attempting to play football in a technical and imaginative way, they're naive but very capable, and it's easy to see a case for the side being really quite strong with a little more experience. Walley, though, stepped down after the tournament, seeing little realistic prospect of continuing his adventure any further.

"It's cost me a lot of money," he admitted. "I realised when I turned up that the stuff it had been agreed they would give me while I was there, that wouldn't last. It had been about two weeks, and it was obvious they'd run out of money. I was financing the team with travel and lunches and stuff like that. It adds up, over a few months."

"I also had to fly in and out of South Africa, as if I'd flown straight into Zimbabwe, I might have been told to bugger off at the airport, or arrested or something. All that travel, in and out of Johannesburg, the hotels, the buses, that came to hundreds of dollars. It was very promising over there for a few months, though. The atmosphere changed completely for a few months. I'm a bit fearful after the [2018 Zimbabwean] elections, but everyone felt different for a while."

Despite the air of hope, Walley kept his head down. "I walked around as a tourist, because things were a bit volatile. There were almost no tourists there, but a volunteer visa was too expensive. I was lying low for some of it, worried that being caught with a British passport, I might be seen as a spook or something. I've had mostly very good experiences with travel, though."

"I wouldn't go to the Democratic People's Republic of Congo by myself, because it would scare the shit out of me, but1 I've been to some pretty dangerous places, and usually they just leave you to it. If you travel wisely, it's often actually safer than at home," he explained. "Once I get out on the road and in the zone, I feel quite confident."

The footballer's journey was more difficult than just the financial and kit restrictions, too: Matabeleland had some trouble getting visas, but they are visibly growing. A sign of the different world the side live in, perhaps, came in the announcement of a women's team shortly after the London tournament.

The move looked quite progressive, especially by the standards of a fringe African football team, but it was followed a few weeks later by the donation of a set of sewing machines to that team, something which somewhat undermined the positive, gender-equality vibe around the entire concept.

In London, though, entirely different problems were emerging.

"In Zimbabwe, you can't even see the pitch markings, you can't see where the half way line is a lot of the time. Setting yourself up with an offside trap, defending that last line, all that stuff is very difficult to coach in Zimbabwe, actually," Walley said of the contrast between Matabeleland's previous experience and their CONIFA play. "They kind of learnt on their feet in London. We developed in the tournament, I think."

"With the Padania game," Walley said of Matabeleland's 6-1 opening day defeat, "you'd have expected a team that's never played anyone at anywhere near that level to go out and get an absolute thrashing. We scored in the second half and came into the game. We had two one on ones with their goalkeeper, too. That could have been 6-3 in the end, and we gifted them a couple of terrible goals. I thought it was very respectable. We grew into things as the tournament went on, too."

"It was like a back to front pyramid, how we did it," Walley concludes as he looks back at the entire process. "There was a huge amount of money raised, especially by my friends. The best part of $25,000 just from friends, and lots of strangers from all around the world helped, too. Then the volunteers came in, and people like CNN Africa and Paddy Power got involved on the media side. We got huge media coverage. There's all these layers of people helping us, playing into us getting to London."

"I'd said to the team, when we go out to London, we've got to express ourselves. Apart from the games, we've got to go over and show everyone who we are. I've always hated how players will stand on the half way line and clap fans. Why can't they come down and do it? We're not different, or special. I tried to get that through to my players. We went and spoke to the fans at the end, and met with them. That's Matabeleland, that's who the team are. They realised that's a good thing to do."

"I don't think any other team playing at anything like that kind of level have ever gone and shaken hands with all the crowd like our players did after the Padania game. That's just who they are."

Ellan Vannin: The Fight for Footballing Identity on a Small Island...

Founded: 2013 Record Win: 14-0 v Chagos Islands Record Loss: 5-1 v Occitania Distance Travelled to London: 258 miles (415 kms) Home Capital: Douglas, Isle of Man Player Pool Playing In: England, Isle Of Man CONIFA Ranking: 4

As far as footballing identity goes, if you take a little step back, the UK might just be the most convoluted place in the world. Formed in a different era (or, in fact, founded from almost any status other than as the founders of international football), England, Scotland, Wales and Northern Ireland would likely compete as just one team. Modern-day footballing convention would require it. Instead, they compete as four, and the rivalry between the sides and their fans is notorious.

That's not all, either. There are various footballing spins offs: Yorkshire are a member of CONIFA and playing increasingly regularly. A Cornish team and a Sussex team are also mooted, and the Channel Islands - regular competitors in the Island Games - have also expressed their footballing identity in various different forms over the years.

The Isle of Man's status is perhaps the most confusing. Few people born on the island - there are a huge number of modern-day arrivals - would consider themselves English. The Isle of Man's status is that of a 'crown dependency'. It's not part of the UK or the EU, but, confusingly, its head of state is the Queen of England, and the UK takes full responsibility for its defence.

In most aspects of life, this convoluted set up has worked out quite well for the approximately 80,000 residents. They pay astonishingly low rates of tax (the top income tax is only 20%, and individual's payments are capped at €120,000 a year). They have one of the highest GDPs in the world. They also pay no inheritance tax, and have an unemployment rate of about 1%.

Despite the convoluted political setup, from a footballing perspective, the Isle of Man Football Association is affiliated with the English Football Association as a 'county', a concept that holds some weight in the English system, but only in a very amateur sense. Since 1890, the very earliest days of international football, the hypothetical route to international football for a Manx person has been wearing England's three lions, despite the fact that the island is not even in the UK. Not that a Manx player has ever succeeded in pulling on England's colours.

A strange consequence of all this has been the need to create a second representative football association on the island, alongside the Isle of Man FA. Ellan Vannin came into being at a time when, arguably, the Isle of Man were in a position to join UEFA, according to the regulations in place. Nevertheless, they gravitated towards CONIFA-style representative football.

When I met Malcolm Blackburn, chairman of the Manx IFA, in London he quickly outlined the situation the team faced. "It's about expressing our identity," he explained. "We're not English, so the set up in place doesn't really work for us. The Isle of Man FA wouldn't be allowed to play in a competition like this. CONIFA allows us to play as we are."

Blackburn also expressed a desire to bring the Isle of Man into UEFA, following in the footsteps of Gibraltar, in particular. He wasn't optimistic about making any progress, though, pointing to a verdict that had seen Jersey rejected earlier in the year.

Jersey's attempt to grab official UEFA recognition has, perhaps, been the most significant European attempt at breaking through to international football in recent years, Gibraltar aside, and has a knock-on effect on almost every entity striving for recognition in the region.

Freedom of Information requests revealed the extent of Jersey's efforts. They undertook multiple trips to Geneva, London and Manchester as they explored the options when it comes to gaining international status. They're also known to have lobbied hard in the build up to a vote about their inclusion in early 2018, pointing to the newly established Nations League as the perfect opportunity to integrate Jersey as a 56th UEFA member, with the nice added bonus that it would even up the eight-team tiered format.

When UEFA congress met to discuss the matter in February, they did so only because the Court of Arbitration for Sport had instructed them to. Jersey's success was always a long shot. In the end, only one UEFA member formally abstained on Jersey's application, while the other 49 of 50 eligible voters chose to go against it. England, interestingly, had decided not to back the bid.

"Jersey cannot be considered as an independent state. The Jersey FA does not satisfy the admission criteria," UEFA president Aleksander Ceferin said at the time. "We are ready to modernise and ready to change football, but we are not above our own statutes."

"This is a big change and a big difference. It would not be in line with our statutes [which require UN recognition] for the Jersey FA to be admitted as a member of UEFA."

Jersey's response was to point to what they saw as the hypocrisy of the decision, and emphasize the negatives for local football, where 13 local teams are lacking broader competition. Their semi-formalised international side is typically limited to one or two games a year.

"We have our own parliament, our own government, our own laws and our own taxes," Jersey FA president Phil Austin told the BBC. "We are recognised by the OECD as a self-governing nation." Self-governing in most term's, but not in footballing ones.

"Around 11% of the membership do not meet the requirements of article five [UEFA's official admission criteria]," Austin pointed out. "If necessary, can't Jersey be added to that list?"

Gibraltar and the Faroe Islands are both amongst the UEFA recognised nations that don't technically meet the requirements for UEFA membership, but the big difference is also an arbitrary one: they got in before the recent rule change. Jerseys' exclusion is very bad news for the Isle of Man, whose status is close to identical to their fellow islanders. The rule, it seems, is now a kind of 'possession is nine tenths of the law' situation.

UEFA is not the only option that's been considered by places facing this kind of situation. Guernsey - another entity of very similar status to the Isle of Man - formed an island side, Guernsey FC in 2011. They had previously had some success in the 2011 UEFA Regions Cup, and decided they'd like to play together more regularly. Guernsey FC went into the English non-league pyramid, where the early days saw consecutive promotions up to the 8th tier of English football, where they now reside, offering a difficult but alluring away day for fans of the likes of Ramsgate and Greenwich Borough.

There are issues with the inclusion of Guernsey, not least in the travel involved for other low-level, amateur clubs in playing against them. There's clearly an interest, though: the record attendance for the club is comfortably over 4,000 - monstrous for that level of English football - and the playing squad is also far deeper than most.

Ellan Vannin, the Isle of Man's alternative, CONIFA side, had looked at a similar 'domestic inclusion' model in the early days. While they weren't willing to reveal who they were discussing inclusion with, a consensus of rumours and oblique references seem to indicate that Ellan Vannin were angling for a place in the League of Ireland, the Republic of Ireland's professional league, when they looked at options for launching a team in 2016.

At the time, then Director of Football Dave Crennel told Irish sports website The42.ie "The association who we're looking to jump on board with seem very keen and are excited about the project, as we are about taking it to that association."

"We can produce footballers that can compete with some of the bigger countries around us. We have done it. We can point to these players and say look, Kieran Tierney, Young Player of the Year in Scotland."

"St George's have been the dominant team (in the Isle of Man), they've won every major trophy comfortably, winning games 5, 6 or 7-0. Attendances are down, people are not excited about it."

"Not to take anything away from St George's achievements, but we want to be able to help people make a living out of the game. We want to help grassroots football progress and that was really the idea behind [trying to join an off-island league]." The change hasn't materialised.

There are side issues to not being able to play international football, of course. CONIFA is not recognised by UEFA, naturally, and so when it comes to call ups, its players are treated very differently by the clubs they're contracted to. Despite the unconventional approach, bringing the best Isle of Man players into a single league side might make sense in terms of pushing a case, and would have the fringe benefit of ensuring the players are available for any such internationals.

As it was, the London 2018 Ellan Vannin side's 23-man squad was hit late on by withdrawals, with Seamus Sharkey (a central defender who plays with Irish club Sligo Rovers) unable to travel, as his club refused permission at late notice after another player in his position got injured. For a full international, Sligo wouldn't have had the option. Conor Doyle, who plays amateur football in Dubai for the incredibly named 'Slugs & Goats FC', was also unable to return and compete.

Despite the issues in getting the preferred team together, Ellan Vannin had finished second at CONIFA's first tournament back in 2014, and were highly optimistic about their chances of making some serious inroads in London.

Frank Jones, the side's captain, gave his view to Isle of Man Weekly ahead of the tournament:

"The mood in the camp is great. It's mainly made up with Corinthians and St George's lads who have all been flying towards the end of the season," he explained.

"It's not great that players like Seamus, Liam Doyle and Conor Doyle can't make it, then there were last-minute pull outs with injuries. However, it's a very strong squad and it's giving young lads the chance to step up to the plate on the 'big stage'. Players like Sean

Doyle, Ste Whitley and Dan Simpson have all been in great form for Corinthians, so I just hope they can carry it into this competition.

"Results wise I would be hoping to get out the group then just see from there - quarter-finals, semi-final and the final, one game at a time."

"It's been a long, drawn-out season after a terrible start with weather, meaning loads of games towards the end. It's not helped with a few of the players missing out with injuries. On the other hand, if you are fit there is nothing better than game time, so it could help us in London with being match sharp."

"All in all, I think we have a good squad and I'm sure all the players will give 100 percent. That's all the coaching staff can ask for and that will take us as far as possible - hopefully winning it."

The two sides that make up most of the squad, Corinthians and St George's, are both interesting outfits in their own right.

Jones' traditionally dominant St George's side are the former side of Ellan Vannin manager Chris Bass Jnr, and play on a ground that doubles as a campsite and has strong associations with the Isle of Man TT bike race.

Corinthians, also from island capital Douglas, are their main modern-day rivals and won two of the islands three major footballing trophies in 2018, somewhat against St George's traditional dominance.

Wherever they might choose to place their loyalties, their football is still inspired largely by the British version of the game: punchy, direct, and effective. From the islander's perspective, though, they're not represented, because they're not English. They're certainly not an English county. CONIFA is their way out.

Matchday 3: Crunch Time, and the Passions of Kabylia

There's only one place to be on matchday three, somehow both the midway points, and only the fourth day since CONIFA 2018 got underway. That's Enfield. The big draw is a crunch match between Northern Cyprus and Abkhazia, a game likely to eliminate one of the early favourites after Karpatalya put both under pressure by taking four points from their two games against the pair.

It's the fans of Kabylia, though, in town for the early game, who immediately draw the eye. Kabylia need a win against Western Armenia to stand any chance of progressing - a result that would be a miracle of sorts, given they lost their opening game 8-0 to CONIFA World number one Panjab in Slough. Western Armenia top the group, yet it's the blue and yellow halved flags of the northern Algerian region that dominate the stands and the feel of the game.

I'd heard about this Berber passion before. A fan at a game earlier in the week had told me of an encounter with the group earlier in his life. Having spent some time traveling in the north of Algeria, he recognised that someone serving him in a north African fast-food joint in London was probably of Berber Algerian origin. On asking, he'd been greeted with hugs and excitement at the specific recognition. Having made friends, he wasn't allowed to pay for anything in that particular takeaway for over a year.

Sat in the back of Enfield's cafe-cum-main-stand, I soon get talking to one of the fans in yellow and blue. As we speak, rows of Kabylians dance passionately to a boombox they've set up in their midst.

"I couldn't play this music when I was young," the Kabyle supporter explains of the twirling melodies. "It was banned in our country. If I was caught listening to it, I'd have been arrested. Berbers have been repressed for a long time, and this movement is quite new. For a lot of people, this is our first real experience of pride in who we are, and we don't care if we win or lose. We care that we get to be here."

A few minutes into the game, the dancing intensifies. Despite needing a win to have any chance of progressing (it turns out they'd have needed a big win, with results elsewhere), Kabylia offer little on the pitch, but the party goes on.

Eventually, my new friend grabs me by the arm and points excitedly at a man who's arriving slightly lower down Enfield's tiny seated stand, and causing quite a stir as he does so. Ferhat Mehenni is a former folk singer, and current President of The Provisional Government of Kabylia in exile. "This is the man whose music I couldn't listen to," he explains in stunned recognition. "He is our leader."

Mehenni watches on quietly for a few minutes, his security detail ensuring nobody gets too close to the seat hastily cleared to one side of the partying fans. My neighbour has now whipped out a book of Mehenni's writing from his bag, and is trying to pluck up the courage to take it down the stand and try to persuade the pair of bulky adjacent guards to let him ask for an autograph. I later look up the music that's blasting in the background. Even when he wrote the songs, it's clear Mehenni had unapologetically strong views on Berber nationhood. His song titles include 'Berber Songs of Struggle and Hope' and 'Hymn to Kabylia'.

The passion is intense, but also mellowed slightly, at least in its numbers, by the game taking place in London. "If this game was in France," another man in yellow leans over to tell me, "We'd be playing in front of thousands. There are not many of us in London. It's a small community here, but this is important to us, because it's so rare to see Kabylia represented like this."

On the pitch, things aren't going so well for the North Algerian side. They're young and a little naive, and don't look like they've played together a great deal. The more experienced Western Armenian squad is outthinking the energetic Algerians, and offer an efficient, effective passing approach as they pile on the pressure.

Arman Mosoyan opens the scoring for the men in orange early on, just as the Kabylian party was getting underway, though the score causes barely a blip in the dancing. His goal comes as the result of consistent pressure and is fired in from a tight angle after a series of attacks on the Kabylia backline.

The Armenians were dominant, in fact, but relatively poorly supported. When Kabylia did get a rare foray forward, they snuck a ball beyond the casual Armenian goalkeeper to equalise, only to be correctly flagged offside. They did finish the first half on top, but were in for a poor start to the second half, with Vigen Valenza-Berberian breaking in from the left wing to net from close range and put the Western Armenians in total control.

Valenza-Berberian, whose normal hunting ground is the French lower tiers, added an emphatic feel to the scoreline late on, as he and Vahagn Militosyan of Slovak side FC Nistra added two very late goals, the first after Armenia smacked the post from a free kick, and the second a classy effort on the break, finished into the roof of the net. The Armenians aren't spectacular, but they are efficient. The Kabylie side have been well beaten, but are passionately and emphatically applauded from the pitch.

Kabylian footballers - or rather footballers who can trace some kind of Kabylian routes - include Zinedine Zidane, Samir Nasri and Karim Benzema, so the potential is clearly quite substantial.

Western Armenia, it turns out, represent an even larger community than the popular and colourful Kabyles. Hiratch Yagan, the man behind the formation of the team, told me "our association is based in Geneva, but we are a very large community in Europe and all over the world. There are more than 13 million Western Armenians in the diaspora."

Western Armenia lies within the current borders of Turkey, and the concept is unpopular with Turks. That makes for an interesting contrast with Northern Cyprus, also a big side within CONIFA, who get passionate Turkish support.

At one time, most of the East of Turkey was predominantly populated by people of Armenian origin. That situation continued right up until the Armenian genocide, a systematic killing off and exportation of people of Armenian origin from the area that took place between 1914 and 1923, with a total of around 1.5 million deaths estimated to have taken place. Some consider the event to be second only to the holocaust as an example of systematic and planned extermination of a people and culture.

Naturally, people from Western Armenia ended up pretty much anywhere else, as they fled the Ottoman Empire in search of somewhere they could simply continue to live. While much of this movement took place almost a century ago, the cultural strength of the Western Armenians lives on in a number of other places.

"We created this team because I have a lot of young friends who are like me, natives of Western Armenia, who would like to play together for this country," founder Hirac Yagan explains of his concept. "CONIFA played a big role in helping to create the association and the team. Now, we have more and more requests for players or people who want to join us."

"For recruitment, we had a stage in Bordeaux at the beginning of January with a lot of new players, but taken from amateur leagues, as the others could not join us at that time, whilst playing for their own professional teams. We played against Stade Montois [a French fourth tier team much better known for their identically-named rugby side]. Then in April, we held a team camp and a game against St Priest [also in the French fourth tier] to prepare for tournament selection."

"We have a lot of players to choose from. I played with Stade Nyonnais, in division three in Switzerland, and a lot of our players are taken from Germany, France and Belgium. Generally, the level is division three or division two, but of course the players who play their football in Armenia are division one level. There are only three from there."

Western Armenia's difficulties in competing at CONIFA are familiar, but not insurmountable.

"The biggest problem for us is always finding money, and we try to connect and get help from as many Armenians as we can, to help us to grow," Yagan tells me. "It's not easy, we're sure that some of them don't know of our existence. If they knew about us, they would be sure to help us. Armenians are very united."

There is a spattering of blue, red and orange tricolours in the crowd and the Armenians leap up when they find the net against their passionate but uninspired opposition. It's clear that their aims are somewhat bigger than their politically heavyweight opposition, in terms of progression at the tournament.

There's a playfulness to the Enfield crowd for that opening fixture, even if the occasion is leant real political weight by the presence of Mehenni and his security. In footballing terms, though, the second game has a far weightier feel.

Northern Cyprus and Abkhazia are two of the more serious contenders at CONIFA, and both were expecting to progress deep into the 2018 tournament. The presence of Karpatlaya, a real surprise thorn in the side of the big guns in Group B, has left their final group games a battle for their lives.

Northern Cyprus fans are colourful and exuberant, and boisterous about their identity and status. "I'm from Cyprus, but of course I could never support the team the island has in UEFA," one fan tells me. "I'm not Greek, and that team is Greek. I'm Turkish. I support Turkey, but that's not really where I come from, so this is better. I don't really want to talk about it, though. It makes me angry."

There's no question the Northern Cypriots are passionate, and Abkhazia, equally, are not afraid to make their presence felt. The semi-autonomous region of Georgia were followed by raucous crowds in their home CONIFA World Cup two years ago, and while they're heavily outnumbered in Enfield, they make their presence felt with a droning chant that echoes through the ground throughout the game.

Both sides have some respectable footballing roots. Northern Cyprus can count Muzzy Izzet - born in England to Northern Cypriot parents - amongst players that could hypothetically have played for them at some stage (he played for Turkey instead).

Until the club's dissolution in 1991, Abkhazia boasted Soviet footballing powerhouse FC Dinamo Sokhumi. That club's players included Avtandil Gogoberidze (an important enough player to eventually appear on Georgian national stamps), and Daur Akhvlediani, a player with over 200 Sukhumi appearances who was ultimately killed in the Abkhazia War. The stadium in his hometown of Gagra was named after him.

The days of Soviet football teams being based in this volatile region seem a long time away: following the battle for its control in 1992-1993, it took until 2011 for the region to be formally declared free of landmines.

Throughout the crucial CONIFA contest, numerous green, white and red flags fly over one side of the ground, the Abkhaz fans stood atop some seats and chanting cyclically 'fa la la la la la la la la, ooh Abkhazia' from first to last. The chant might be accompanied by swooping flags and a burst of colour, but it has a sombre feel next to the party that is the Kabylian fans and the passion of the Cypriots; a dreary, droning, sullen anthem converted to the sports field.

The Abkhazian flag, which later turns up in the crowd at FIFA 2018 World Cup games in Kazan, contains an open hand, said to be a greeting to friends, and warning to enemies simultaneously. The green and white stripes represent the area's apparent openness towards cohabiting Christians and Muslims, something that's not lost on some of the Cypriot fans, who seem to embrace the opposition.

The football, though, has reached serious business time, and it's immediately apparent that both these sides comfortably outclass the two that came before them. Abkhazia are a steady, metronomic side, the holders powered by playmaking defensive man Anri Khagush who's extremely competent, if unadventurous, on the ball.

Khagush is a regular at Russian premier league side Arsenal Tula, a former under-21 international whose career has seen stop offs as Spartak Moscow, Rostov and Belarusian side BATE Borisov. At the latter, he even travelled to Real Madrid's Bernabeu in the Champions League, where his side lost 2-0 after he was sent off.

Real Madrid didn't take the contest particularly well - in fact, almost ten years later the Spanish club complained about having had to play BATE, calling it 'not box office' in their critique of the Champions League format (a little harsh, given the Belarusians drew home and away with Juventus that year). It's fair to say Khagush stands out more than a little in Enfield, and the side around him are slick and efficient, if sometimes lacking the decisive pass.

Northern Cyprus are a different sort of team. Their frontman, a former Irish under-21 international born in London, immediately stands out. Billy Mehmet is a fine footballer, technically proficient and dangerous in the air, and happens to look a lot like he'd fit right in should he ever get into boxing. A varied career has taken him from St Mirren and Dunfermline in Scotland (in seven years with the two clubs, he scored a notable 73 goals) to spells at Bangkok Glass and Perth Glory. Around Mehmet, who is getting on a bit in footballing terms, Northern Cyprus are young, fast and attacking.

Mehmet and Halil Turan dominated the early stages and should really have dismissed Abkhazia before the game became too much of a contest, as both missed great chances to have Northern Cyprus in front.

The Cypriot fans were becoming frustrated, and the tension ratcheted up quickly when Abkhazia's first decent attack of the game saw them net, through a curled finish from 25 yards by Torpedo Moscow forward Dmitryi Maskayev.

Unal Kaya's header to level for Northern Cyprus was less spectacular, but certainly deserved on the balance of play, though Abkhazia slammed the crossbar from a freekick just before half time in a contest both sides knew was vital to their chances in the competition.

The second half had a strange dynamic, with the reality of the situation setting in. Northern Cyprus knew a draw would see them through to the second round, though not as group winners, and adopted a more defensive approach. That worked well for at least 20 minutes, with a few bonus chances falling their way on the counterattack.

With Abkhazia forced to push further and further forward, Kenan Oshan hit them on the break to give Northern Cyprus the lead, and leave Abkhazia needing two goals in the closing fifteen minutes. They got one, through a penalty from Vladimir Argun, who did well to ignore playful antics from the Northern Cyprus goalkeeper, and there followed a brief period of intense pressure as Abkhazia at their attempt to retain their title.

It was the Cypriot team, though, who got the result they needed to progress. The holders were third, and out of the running, destined to play for 9th place at best. With 2014 winners County of Nice not present in London, a new World-level CONIFA champion was now guaranteed.

*

Oddly, for a southern Englishman, I don't really know modern London. Much of my journalistic working life has inadvertently gravitated towards the city in recent years. Despite living in Dublin, over half of the publications I work for are based in or around the capital. The last time I spent more than perhaps five days in a row in the UK was shortly after returning from two years in South Korea, in 2008. It's my homeland, but in some very substantial ways, for me it has also become a foreign country. Instead, Ireland has crept permanently into the familial, and Dublin has etched itself on my soul.

For CONIFA, I base myself at my brother's place in Peckham, and quickly learn that the tournament's description of 'London' is quite a loose one. In fact, it probably relates quite closely to an over-enthusiastic estate agent's. I'm spending half my CONIFA experience on public transport, trying to work out the least complex way to transfer between, for example, the two south London districts of Sutton and Bromley (after doing this trip twice, I maintain the best way to cover that particular ten mile gap is walk, though I didn't actually try it), or to get from south London to Enfield, in the north.

I learn that Enfield is London, but only just, and the ground is easily 90 minutes from the city's centre. Haringey is similar, and both involve several transfers to hop to. Sutton United's address claims the club is in Surrey, as does Carshalton's. Bromley seems to be just inside the border of Greater London, and don't get me started on Slough and Bracknell, both of which are so far out, I decide to exclude them from my CONIFA itinerary entirely.

Fisher FC, a phoenix club that's grown in place of former fifth tier club Fisher Athletic, are a happy exception. They have a pitch that looks a lot like a computer-generated fake, backed with a view of towering Canary Wharf just across the Thames, and seem to be the only truly city-based ground in the entire tournament. It doesn't help the travel, of course, that the tournament is being played out in one of London's most impressive heat waves of the last decade, to the distinct advantage of some sides over others.

Most days, I'm rocking into my long-suffering brother's place fairly late at night, I'm spending the evening post-match following that greatest of low-tier sports journalism conventions, chasing players and managers onto the pitch and interrupting their warm down in search of essential interviews and stories.

I'm living on a diet of supermarket sandwiches and stadium fast food, mingling with the muddled assortment of media who've deemed the tournament worthy of their attention: the Guardian and Vice, occasionally, but more regularly a heap of little footballing blogs, international political commentators and the occasional viewer in search of something to protest.

It's a weird kind of media mismatch, the tiny outlets' writers clutching notepads and jostling for attention and headline-grabbing tales, and the bigger ones looking for the in-depth, strutting about with high-end cameras and the 'quirky' presenter of the day, who may well be at his first football match this decade.

In truth, I've long been a bit of a cultural wanderer myself, and it does play into my fascination with CONIFA. My wife and I trace the roots of our relationship firmly back to our time living in Seoul. She's from the rural west of Ireland, but we live in relatively metropolitan Dublin. Part of me feels Irish, though my heritage is almost all English, apart from a speck of Irishness a few generations back.

I had a kind, positive and nurturing upbringing, but my dad's job meant I didn't really settle in one place until I was almost a teenager, and so that connection to 'roots' that a lot of people talk about has never really applied to me. The concept of 'home' exists in my psyche, of course, but it doesn't stand tall, particularly. That's probably for the best, as the town I grew up in more than any other, Salisbury - now best known for the Novichok chemical attack - is old-world and beautiful but deeply conservative, populated largely by the elderly, and lacking employment opportunities. Almost everyone I went to school with has left. For me, I guess, my outlook just made that easier.

These things all play into perspective. Travel and life experience has shredded my view of the UK. I think the English education system has a lot to answer for here: in history, for example, I remember going in-depth on World War II and the industrial revolution, as well as the Romans and the Tudors. I can't remember anything more than a glossing over of colonialism, and I think that's appalling. I went to a good school, too, and I arrived in Ireland shockingly ignorant of the extent of the UK's impact on the island, let alone in less touted areas like the Chagos Islands. I suspect that's common, but maybe I was just unlucky.

Nevertheless, for me, it has been hard to spend substantial time and absorb any amount of the history of places like India and Ireland and not feel an aching disconnect and a growing anger with the history of my own country. To top things off, I was literally disenfranchised by the Brexit vote, which, as a Brit living elsewhere in the EU, was always likely to impact me disproportionally more than those who actually could take part. That this has come alongside a rapid-learning of the (obvious, in hindsight) evils of Empire that I feel I should have been taught from the start has hit me hard.

The end result, truthfully, is a feeling of disconnection and frustration. I know who I am, but I don't know where I fit in, nationally speaking. I'm also not sure it actually really matters. My passion for my identity and background has been stripped back substantially by my life's experience to date. I can relate, though, to the pain of those who have had their own place in the world stripped without such a choice, such a gentle but sometimes difficult progression on their views of 'self'. My own journey of personal national identity crisis and confusion is, perhaps, something that sits alongside my love of football as a reason this book came into being. It's been confusing and difficult at times, and I'm not sure I've reached the end of that particularly journey.

At CONIFA, the teams themselves are doing plenty around the tournament to portray their cultures and identities, and they're gloriously easy to access. Most of the non-domestic based sides are shacked up in the same spot in north London, where the basement meeting room has been turned into a spot for debate on fringe national football: how it can be improved, who should be involved (and how), how it should be promoted and any other aspect you care to mention.

The issues on the table are largely about moving forward: where to take the tournament in the future, how to engage with the public, issues around qualification methods, how the hell it's all going to be paid for, and the introduction of the green card. The teams are sharing a single training pitch, and almost universally struggling on various levels of tight budgets, but they're working together to improve their lot, and focusing, much like a charity or human rights organisation, on how they can help each other and all ultimately come out a little better off.

I drop in one day to find an abundance of volunteers and the executive, all dressed in pale blue CONIFA branded polos and smiling their way through it all, presenting themselves to the press. To get to the executive, I simply have to stroll past a vivid technicolour of athletic-looking types occupying the lobby in the colours of various teams attending the tournament, in sharp yellow and black or jagged black and sky blue. Most of the press conferences I attend in my day-to-day life are deadly serious, and at times CONIFA's are no different. The executive are challenged on their political views and their finances, and on how on earth it all works, but their passion shines through it all.

"We've nothing against FIFA," Sascha Duerkop says in one particularly comic answer about the more high-profile purveyor of international football. "They are very great to learn how not to do things."

Before they speak, the organisation takes the chance to show off, subtly, some of the quirky sides of the World Football Cup. Right Said Fred, the brothers of 'I'm Too Sexy' fame, deliver the tournament song, which runs on a YouTube video on the big screen, alongside clips of the matches so far. 'Bring Down The House' is the kind of slightly-silly Europop track that gets wedged in your head, with lyrics around inclusivity which take gentle stabs at FIFA along the way. "Sing your own song," the band screams, against a backdrop of low-tier football and clever camera tricks.

Mark Clattenburg, who's been shipped in from his current refereeing role in the Middle East, is taking charge of some of the higher profile games, and his team's use of the green card is another hot topic. It's generally popular, and revolutionary enough to draw attention from the likes of Sky Sports.

The north London student accommodation does touch on one of the great conventions of tournament football: squad boredom. The players might be stepping onto the astros almost every day in the early stages of the tournament, but inside their accommodation, there are entire squads of players draped over the seats in reception, fiddling with phones or joking around with computer games. Sat in their team tracksuits, they look like they're waiting for something to happen, killing time until another of the assigned buses pulls up outside to drag them through the London traffic to take on their next opponent. Boredom might be pervasive, but the squad jokes, at least, seem to have been kept behind closed doors.

The games are all being streamed live on the internet, which does give coaches a sense of the playing style and quality of their future, or prospective opposition. The consensus early on seems to

101

be that Padania are the team to beat, with a couple of other strong sides - particularly Northern Cyprus, Panjab and Szekely Land - looking like serious contenders.

Matabeleland, meanwhile, have started a different kind of fundraising. The replica team shirts have been distributed, and are proving fiercely popular around the grounds, appearing on the touchline of almost every game.

The Zimbabwean side have turned their attention to the single day they have to enjoy after the tournament finishes: in between the training with Bruce Grobbelaar, getting used to the pitches and a growing shirt distribution network, they're trying to add to their 'once in a lifetime' for the players, and fund some London sightseeing.

*

Around the grounds, news is coming in of who's marching on, and who's falling into the placement stage of the World Football Cup. Group A is perhaps the most intense: while Cascadia battle hard against a goal difference disadvantage in their game with the group's strugglers Tamil Eelam, Barawa are fighting for their very existence in the tournament they're hosting. The Somali hosts know they probably need a win against Ellan Vannin to stand any real chance of progression.

Barawa look more like the side that turned out on the opening night, as they play controlled football from the off in Haringey. Ellan Vannin, though, create several early chances, their fiery shirt fading from red to orange in the north London sunshine, and their football looking promising.

Barawa are edging back into the game before half time, and take the lead through former Libyan international Mohamed Bettamer, who hits a potent first time shot from outside the area into the Manx men's net.

Bettamer threatens to add another after half time, missing two solid chances, but it's his shot that creates a key rebound, calmly slotted in by Shaquille Ismail midway through the second period. The second goal pushes Barawa ahead of their opponents on goal difference.

Ellan Vannin pile on the pressure, and both sides are forced into changes through green cards. The Manx side have a late call for a penalty, but Barawa hold on, and the 2-0 win ensures they progress and achieve their pre-tournament target of a quarter final. Several of their players celebrate by dropping to the grass and praying, having come through the late-match tiring effects of their limited Ramadan diet.

The result means Cascadia need to score six in the simultaneous game against Tamil Eelam at Fisher FC, in order to overcome the Ellan Vannin side's goal difference and grab second place. The result in Haringey, in fact, not only eliminates the Tamils, but is about as bad as it could be for the Americans' chances.

They take the lead from an early penalty from Jon Nouble, though Tamil Eelam were creating some decent opportunities at the other end, too, in an open game in front of a small number of boisterous American fans. Tayshon Haden-Smith's volley putting the west coast side 2-0 up before half time probably slightly flatters them.

The news was filtering through from Haringey, though, and it already looked likely Cascadia would need at least five goals to go through, an almighty demand even against the weakest team in the group. They came out in the second half with that in mind, attacking from the off.

With the ball pinballing around the Tamil's penalty area early in the second half, the third goal came from Yuri Farkas after a smooth break, and the fourth came along not too much later, with Hayden-Smith finishing off a pacey break and precise cross.

Things looked to have been derailed, though, as news of the second goal for Barawa came through to Fisher, and defender Matt Braem was sent from the pitch, leaving Cascadia a man short. Showing plenty of stoic resilience, however, the Americans - who had grown through the tournament as they forged a team from their disparate parts - went on to pull off a minor miracle.

First, Jon Nouble spun a strike from the corner of the penalty area into the Tamil's top corner, before immediately charging in to reclaim the ball from the Tamil's net and sprint back to the centre circle. Finally, Calum Ferguson secured their progression in the dying seconds, sliding home on the break against a tiring Tamil defence. The 6-0 win gave the Americans a goal difference one better than Ellan Vannin, and saw them through to the quarter finals in the tightest group in CONIFA history. The story of this particular group, though, wasn't quite over.

Elsewhere in Abkhazia and Northern Cyprus' group B, Karpatalya had reasserted the strength signalled in getting results out of the group's two favourites, comfortably putting away Tibet in Bracknell. The Ukrainian/ Hungarian side were on top from the off, with Zsolt Gaidus scoring very early, and the men in red adding two more before half time.

Karpatalya would ultimately beat the Asian side 5-1, but the well-supported Tibetans did grab another goal, through Pema Lhundup, whose lobbed finish from 25 yards bamboozled Karpatalya's impressive goalkeeper Béla Fejér. Karpatalya's win ensured the late addition to the tournament topped group B, over two of the early favourites, and Abkhazia dropped into the placement half of the draw.

In group C, things had become a question of position, and preferred quarter final opponents by the end of matchday two. Two of the favourites, Padania and Szekely Land, faced off in a battle to win the group. Szekely Land opened well, smashing the crossbar through the dangerous Istvan Fülop after only two minutes, and generally looking very much in charge of the early stages.

Instead of going in front, though, they twice made a hash of things at the back, allowing Gianluca Rolandone to nod in Padania's first decent attack of the game unmarked, and then Giacomo Innocente to nick the ball from a bumbling defender and score from close range. The third wasn't great, either, as the Szekely 'keeper

Barna Nágy couldn't keep hold of a cross, and let an easy header past him into the net.

The Padanians had already proven ruthless, and Szekely Land's profligacy gave them a mountain to climb and the north Italians what was, on the balance of play, an ill-deserved 3-0 lead. Still, the Szekely fans were fast becoming one of the sights of the tournament, and as their abundant flares came back out, they began to have an impact.

The boisterous Hungarians won a penalty early in the second half, but Barna Bájka slammed it against the crossbar. They finally got some reward late on, Lászlo Szocs hit the net with a late consolation. All that meant Padania had won the group, but Szekely Land had every bit as much cause for optimism heading into the knock outs games, despite a 3-1 defeat.

The game, played in the tiny ground of Combined Counties League Premier Division side Bedfont Sports FC (who play in level nine of the English football pyramid) had kicked off to the sound of a beautiful soprano version of Padania's anthem, but closed out to a raucous self-styled sing-along from the Hungarian fans despite their loss.

For the football romantics, though, the other game in the group, between two of the tournament's minnows, held a lot of appeal. Between them, Tuvalu - who trained for CONIFA by making use of the South Pacific Islands' airport runway in-between relatively rare landings - and the Zimbabwean region of Matabeleland had scored one goal and conceded 23 over their first two games. This final group game was probably their best chance to get a victory before the closing stages of the placement rounds.

The game, in truth, was a love in. Matabeleland star and captain Shylock Ndlovu scored the first at Haringey Borough in a contest that wasn't strong from either side defensively, but offered endless entertainment. Ndlovu calmly slid the ball home from eight yards after a nice bit of build-up play from the African side in the tribal-patterned shirts.

Tuvalu had created little up to that point, and were wide open defensively, offering little resistance to Matabeleland's pacey forward play as they seemed to lack structure. They defended largely individually, allowing Matabeleland to play the ball around them. They got back into the game, though, through Etimoni Timuani, whose firm finish into the roof of the net was Tuvalu's first goal of the tournament.

From there on, the well-drilled Matabeleland side took control, with Ndlovu's speed again beating the Tuvalu backline to allow him to slot home at the back post as he was played in with a fine cross-field ball past the Tuvalu goalkeeper. Ndlovu was denied a hattrick by a sharp penalty save shortly afterwards, with Katepu Iosua in the Tuvalu goal guessing the right way after a diving handball on the ground from one of his despairing full backs.

Tuvalu pushed on, looking for an equaliser, but were undone at the back again with another penalty late on to give Matabeleland a 3-1 win. The game was only relevant in determining placement round opponents, but clearly attracted a lot of affection from those on the pitch and off it. Matabeleland players embraced their Tuvalu counterparts at the final whistle, before bowing in front of their colourful supporters and dancing from the pitch, their faces plastered in smiles.

"We've just beaten a country," manager Justin Walley said later. "I couldn't be more proud."

In group D, however, there was some more significant action still to come, with all four sides still able to qualify for the sharp end of the remaining action. I'd already seen Western Armenia swat aside Kabylia, in front of a crowd passionately disposed towards the losing side, a result which changed little for the other two sides in the group. Panjab needed a draw to get past a United Koreans In Japan side that was yet to score or concede a goal in the opening two games.

Panjab had scored 8 in their opener, but lost some momentum as they were beaten by the Armenians in their Slough 'home' venue in the second match. The south Asian diaspora side always looked in charge, however, as they booked their place in the next round.

The Zainichi Koreans (the nickname the side choose to represent their Japanese status, meaning 'settled Korean foreigners') had goalkeeper Woo Dae Shim to thank for their opening draws, having largely been on the back foot in the first two games. Soon, they had his diving save up high - pulled off as his body moved the other way from an early Gurjit Singh penalty - to add to the increasingly long list of the young 'keeper's contributions.

The Koreans grew into the contest, however, threatening to silence the rapid-fire Punjabi drum beats around the Slough ground as they went full on towards the Panjab goal in the closing stages of the first half, with Ken Taniyama bouncing a threatening shot along the top of the crossbar.

A messy second half contest finally saw the deadlock broken by Amar Purewal, scorer in the 2016 final, also from the penalty spot, to give Panjab a 1-0 lead and a two-goal cushion on their qualification.

The United Koreans were the only team yet to notch a goal in the tournament until they equalised very late on, with a thundering strike from Su Hyeon Mun in the 94th minute to secure the east Asians' third draw in three games. The bullet finish wasn't enough to pull the Koreans through - it barely allowed time for them to kick off and look for the necessary second, either - but it was a bullet of a strike. Panjab progressed in second place, with the late goal of no consequence to their tournament.

Of the four groups, two had gone almost to the wire, while two had seen clear qualifiers emerge at the earliest possible stage. There had been clear stand outs, in goal-hungry Padania, Szekely Land and Karpatalya. Panjab and Ellan Vannin had started strongly, then faded, while Cascadia had grown into the tournament and holders Abkhazia had crashed out after never really taking off.

United Koreans In Japan had been reliably proficient at the back and weak at the front, though they'd also scored the goal of the tournament late on. Then there'd been whipping boys: Tamil Eelam,

Matabeleland, Tuvalu and Kabylia weren't quite up to the task, at least when it came to the bigger games. For those smaller sides, taking part was a bigger deal. Every game had been an experience, each laden with its own lively brand of passion and colour.

Day Three Results (Sunday, June 3)

Group A

Barawa 2 – 0 Ellan Vannin
Cascadia 6 – 0 Tamil Eelam

Final standings:

Barawa	**6 (+5 goal difference)**
Cascadia	**6 (+4)**
Ellan Vannin	6 (+3)
Tamil Eelam	0 (-12)

Group B

Abkhazia 2 -2 Northern Cyprus
Karpatalya 5 – 1 Tibet

Final standings:

Karpatalya	**7 (+6)**
Northern Cyprus	**5 (+2)**
Abkhazia	4 (+1)
Tibet	0 (-9)

Group C

Padania 3 – 1 Szekely Land
Tuvalu 1 – 3 Matabeleland

Final standings:

Padania	9 (+15)
Szekely Land	6 (+7)
Matabeleland	3 (-8)
Tuvalu	0 (-14)

Group D

Western Armenia 4 – 0 Kabylia
Panjab 1 – 1 United Koreans In Japan

Final standings:

Western Armenia	7 (+5)
Panjab	4 (+7)
United Koreans	3 (0)
Kabylia	1 (-12)

Controversy Hits: Ellan Vannin go to War with CONIFA

It's an off day from the tournament, and I'm trying to check out of it all a little, as well as doing some casual preparation for the knockout stages. In fact, I'm halfway through another public transport nightmare in trying to get from South London to Legoland Windsor, to give my wife and four-year-old some richly deserved family time. I'm somewhere around Slough, dipping into the local Indian cuisine and waiting for a bus that seems to have given up the ghost, as a battle from behind the scenes, one that threatens to blight the tournament in the public eye, suddenly breaks out from its cover and into a very public Twitter spat.

Ellan Vannin, the Isle of Man side, are - alongside 2016's champions Abkhazia - the big, unexpected early departure from the group stages. Having won their opening two games against Cascadia and a weak Tamil Eelam side, the Manx side looked strong favourites to progress as group winners ahead of Sunday's round of matches, in which they faced hosts Barawa.

The Manx side would have been strong favourites to qualify ahead of that game, but they lost. Having failed to dispatch a fairly weak Tamil Eelam side by the same emphatic scores their group rivals managed, they headed out of the sharp end of the competition on goal difference, despite winning six points. They were a bit unlucky: six points is the maximum it's possible to earn in this format of tournament football and still fail to progress.

Ellan Vannin, of course, are a side at the very heart of CONIFA from the very outset. They've appeared at every tournament so far aside from the one held in Abkhazia (they'd qualified, but pulled out for safety reasons, having been advised not to travel by the British Home Office).

When Yorkshire were looking for early opponents after joining CONIFA, Ellan Vannin were the side that stepped up to give them their first game. The organisation was even secondarily formed on the island with a set up in Douglas, due to the commitment the side had shown to the concept over the years.

The day after their defeat and third place in the group finish, the side become quite vocally and aggressively unhappy on social media. Their anger is directed at CONIFA in general, but also with general secretary Sascha Duerkop in particular.

The main issue Ellan Vannin found fault with was the inclusion of former Libyan international Mohamed Bettamer in the Barawa squad, a decision they felt was made too late to allow the player to compete. It certainly came far after the initial squad announcement. Bettamer had been a key player in Ellan Vannin's defeat, scoring one goal and setting up the other as Barawa came out 2-1 on top, a result that combined with Cascadia's thumping late goal fest against Tamil Eelam combined to eliminate the Manx side.

Bettamer, admittedly, also isn't from Barawa, but neither are much of the squad. Their focus is more on the broader Somali diaspora, and the inclusion of players that have links to the diaspora in the UK, a category into which Bettamer and several of their other players fall. Given CONIFA can't exactly check passports in such a scenario (how do you prove your roots in places like Tibet, Abkhazia, Padania or Tamil Eelam?), these things are treated much more loosely.

There's no CONIFA rule formally giving the consequences of 'fielding an ineligible player' in CONIFA's rulebook, but Ellan Vannin are convinced Bettamer is just that, because of his late registration. They take the view the result between the two sides should be rewritten as an automatic 3-0 win to Ellan Vannin, as per both footballing convention, and long-established FIFA regulations. Such a result, had it been granted, would have seen them through top of their group, and into the quarter finals.

As the story unfolds, it becomes clear that both sides have a substantial case for their actions. Ellan Vannin hadn't been informed of Mohamed Bettamer's inclusion, though CONIFA say it was sanctioned at a date they had deemed acceptable under the circumstances. There was little doubt amongst teams collectively that Bettamer was announced after the initial squad deadline of May 15th. Cascadia, who had qualified from the group in second place, but also faced Bettamer the day before, were said to be unhappy too. They didn't go so far as to come out publicly and say so, but informally, those close to the side were making clear noises.

CONIFA, it turned out, agreed that the player was added to Barawa's squad late, but argue that the rules have to be quite lax in order for the tournament to go ahead. They admit to an error, but only in communication.

The organisation's argument makes far more sense than it would in the context of a normal football tournament: there are countless reasons why squad lists might change at late notice at CONIFA that simply wouldn't apply at a more high-profile, professional tournament.

Some teams don't have the funds to book travel until a few days before they depart (Matabeleland, for example, rely on a loan from manager Justin Walley's mum). Others have to switch squad lists around at late notice due to problems with visas, or late permission from clubs over players availability, or for countless other reasons to do with politics and personal circumstance.

Ellan Vannin themselves had intended to have a centre back called Seamus Sharkey in their squad, but his Irish league team Sligo Rovers refused to release him at late notice due to their own defensive crisis. The club were not obliged to do let Sharkey go, as CONIFA is not formally recognised as international football, and so regulations requiring a player be released don't apply. Sharkey was replaced. The CONIFA view, essentially, was that there had to be some flexibility in some rules to allow a tournament to happen at all.

Nonetheless, Ellan Vannin were livid. "I can't believe what's happened at the CONIFA World Cup," team captain Frank Jones posted on his Twitter account. "All our hard work and money spent to make sure we got to London and do our best, to get done over by rule breaking." He throws in an accusation of corruption, too.

Ellan Vannin also release an extended and cutting statement, outlining the situation from their view. Bettamer - a former African Champions League and African Cup of Nations star - was added to the Barawa squad following their opening day 4-0 win against Tamil Eelam, with the consent of the organising committee, but without the knowledge of other teams.

In their view, this is entirely unacceptable, and the Manx side decide to go nuclear, and quit the tournament entirely. A long, scathing statement from Ellan Vannin announces their departure, taking issue with multiple aspects of the decision. Some highlights include the following:

"Ellan Vannin seriously dispute that this decision was taken by the organising committee. It was a unilateral decision by the General Secretary," they argue. "CONIFA have advised that the majority of teams did not provide their squad list by May 28, as required."

At a meeting, they continue, "Ellan Vannin were given the chance to present their case, which included stating that Ellan Vannin had come to the tournament with only 22 players, as one pulled out at the last minute, and at the first game had four players who were injured and unlikely to take any further part in the tournament. If Ellan Vannin had been aware of an unsanctioned rule change, they would have had every right to fly in replacement players."

The situation is not helped by news breaking that Ellan Vannin had initially won an appeal in an emergency meeting, with Barawa's games against both Ellan Vannin and Cascadia re-cast at 3-0 defeats. The decision was then reversed a few hours later in a vote of participating teams, in favour of Barawa.

"Why has this situation been manipulated by CONIFA?" Ellan Vannin continue in their statement on the off day. "It's obvious Barawa are the hosts, and to correctly sanction them under the tournament rules would result in them not progressing to the quarter finals, reducing the appeal of the tournament and financial gain against what can be achieved by little Isle of Man with limited support progressing."

It's worth noting that the financial argument doesn't particularly ring true: Barawa were not, by any stretch, a well-supported side in London despite being the hosts. There were ample sides with more substantial support bases, ranging from traveling Cascadia to popular Tibet. Northern Cyprus' fan base outnumbered Barawa's by a multiple of at least 50 at the average game.

Ultimately, the men from the Isle of Man decide to withdraw from the remainder of the competition, and CONIFA respond by temporarily suspending them from the organisation, claiming they had brought the tournament into disrepute with their statement. For most, it's a minor shadow over the tournament. CONIFA's stance does go against their rules, but the context is everything.

Looking for that context, I ask Paul Watson, a CONIFA director, about the changes. He says there were more than 25 of them after the formal squad deadlines, and adds that Barawa have offered to withdraw from the tournament over the issue, an offer CONIFA has rejected. Ellan Vannin, perhaps, weren't aware of the flexibility being offered elsewhere. Duerkop later clarifies further online, as part of a bitter Twitter exchange:

"Just to get that straight," he says in response to Ellan Vannin's comments, "the deadline for squad submission was the 26th of May. Twelve of sixteen teams requested changes after that date for injured or visa rejected players, including Ellan Vannin. They got an approval by myself on behalf of the committee and all the teams, including Ellan Vannin played these players."

"If rules are strictly applied, two teams couldn't play at all due to visa issues. Ellan Vannin would have had four less players. In the interests of football, we thus approved to be a bit "soft", as long as no more than 23 players enter the tournament..."

"Admittedly, only that one Barawa player came in after a match was played," he continued. "That's the only difference. The procedure Barawa have taken is no different to the one Ellan Vannin did. The rules where bent for you as they were for them."

"We came to the conclusion that Barawa didn't break any rule at all," Duerkop explained to me later. "What we had to sanction

Ellan Vannin for was refusing to accept the democratic decision of the organisation, which included all the members here."

"They broke four or five points on the code of ethics that they signed before they came here. They put the continuation of the tournament in jeopardy, in that we weren't able to satisfactorily complete the tournament without them in the same way, so we had no choice but to sanction them."

"We couldn't expel them from the tournament in response, as obviously they've chosen not to be there anymore. But we had to take a decision, so we took it to the executive committee and decided to expel them from CONIFA. But all decisions taken by the executive committee at CONIFA are always temporary. Whether it's to admit a new team, to expel a team or to sanction a team, the decision always goes to the AGM."

"At the AGM, every team is present and they have the absolute majority of the votes. Every team had ten votes, and we each have one vote, because we want them to run the organisation. So Ellan Vannin will be invited to present their case and their position and the teams will make the decision. We'll see where it goes from there."

Ellan Vannin were re-admitted at the AGM in early 2019, against the desires of the executive, by member majority.

Onwards in Defeat: the no exit tournament.

"One of my favourite things about the tournament, which is interesting, as I wasn't sure about it before, has been the placement games," Paul Watson said at the pre-final press conference. "They really epitomise what CONIFA is."

I had been similarly unsure as I headed for London. The idea of an expelled national team continuing to play at a conventional international tournament would, almost unquestionably, be met with derision. A play-off game for third and fourth place at major championships is already seen as a footballing afterthought, so the offering of a 13th v 14th, presumably, would go down like a lead balloon.

Then the tournament kicks in. Of course, the glory, and the bigger attendances, all fall at the top end of CONIFA, but there are so many teams here that are celebrating turning up, and the placement matches are allowing them to find their level. For some teams, it's allowing them to play their 4th, 5th and 6th international games ever in London, as well as their debut three.

Tuvalu are a notable example, and their President Soseaua Tinilau is keen to talk up their experience after the competition ends, despite his side having been on the receiving end of some heavy losses.

"We are very happy because we ended up winning the last game of the tournament. We are preparing for the Pacific Games in Samoa, so this is a very good learning experience for them. I said to them 'as long as you learn something from this, that's all we want'," he explained. "We are working towards the Pacific Games"

"Back home we play on natural grass, here is an artificial one. It's my first time to step on one, it's so soft. You can see when the ball bounces, it dies out completely. It's quite an experience for them. Now they are getting the feel of it and they are acclimatizing to it."

"At the moment we are trying to upgrade our playing field back home and I also suggested an artificial surface for the new one, so I think maybe next year we will have a new playing ground. Hopefully, it will meet the criteria they are looking at."

For teams like Tuvalu, every little experience plays into their development, and opens their eyes to opportunities.

Kabylia: the CONIFA Final's most passionate separatists?

Founded: 2017 Record Win: 8-1 v Tibet Record Loss: 8-0 v Panjab Distance Travelled to London: 1052 miles (1693 kms) Home Capital: Bgayet Bejaia, Algeria Player Pool Playing In: Algeria, France, Spain, England, Canada CONIFA Ranking: unranked

The Kabyle people are a Berber indigenous ethnic minority from an area that nobody seems to entirely agree on, aside from to say that it's based around the Tell Atlas Mountains, about 100 miles east of Algiers.

The Kabylian region has a population of around 10 million people, and its politics, particularly that of a burgeoning separatist movement, have long been a cause for substantial concern in Algerian political spheres. Kabylia, one of the poorest and parts of Algeria, would very much like not to be part of the north African country at all.

Currently, the main political representatives of the Kabyle people are MAK (Mouvement pour l'Autodétermination de la Kabylie), a political party that views Algerian governance of the region as a form of annexation. From a Kabyle perspective, there has been a consistent issue with the repression of Kabyle views - in effect, a conflation of what it is to be Algerian and Arabic, and a systematic attempt to repress Berber culture.

Today, Algeria and Kabylia do not recognise each other. Kabylia considers itself to be colonised and a significant part of the population is thought to want to exercise a right to self-determination. In order to deal with the diplomatic successes of the Kabyle Provisional Government, Algiers seems to be painting the Kabylian separatists as a borderline terrorist entity, and seems unwilling to offer many concessions.

Kabylia - or at least the separatists amongst its population - says it's fighting against the attempt from the Algerian government to "Arabise" its children through education, media and the administration. Complaints also touch on economy, and the overwhelming impact of regionalist Algerian tax spending, which include the blocking of economic projects and the refusal of investment authorisations. Its natural resources, including oil, lead, zinc and water are also, in the eyes of Kabyles, abused by the Algerian government

This shopping list of grievances has meant substantial and growing insecurity in the region. Over the past 10 years, more than 100 CEOs, merchants or members of their families have been kidnapped in Kabylia, which in turn has pushed a large number of Kabyle business owners into moving their businesses away from the region due to concerns about their own safety. This, naturally, has further exacerbated the issues with investment into and unemployment in the region. It's also driven a culture of departure of young people, with those who are able typically heading for Europe, or sometimes French-speaking Canada.

In June and July 1998, the region flared up in mass protest, after the assassination of protest singer and political activist Lounès Matoub. This took place around the same time a new law requiring the use of Arabic in all fields of education entered into force, as opposed to the Berber Kabyle language, further worsening tensions.

The problems flared again a few years later. In April 2001 a high school student called Massinissa Guermah died in police custody, leading to major riots in Kabylia. The riots, known as the Black Spring, resulted in 123 deaths and more than two thousand injuries as Algerian authorities tried to shut down protests.

Ultimately, the national government was forced to negotiate with the Arouch, a confederation of ancestral local councils, over the ongoing tension and conflict, a negotiation that also touched on wider issues such as social justice and the economy.

The government saw Kabylia as a danger to national unity, but did take small steps, recognising the Berber language, Tamazight in

2002. As of 7 February 2016, after a campaign of pressure, Tamazight became an official language of the State alongside Arabic, but this felt very late to Kabyles, who continued to complain of forced removal of their culture.

All this tension also spilled over into the football. When the majority of CONIFA squads were announced ahead of the London tournament, the Kabyle one was conspicuous in its absence. The team had been training and playing in secret in Paris, to avoid political consequences, and had chosen not to be identified ahead of the tournament due to the political risk that might be posed to them should they be named.

The players are not drawn from the heights of Kabylia-linked stars, because many simply wouldn't take the risk. Instead, they are drawn mainly from the lower tiers of the French league, though six brave players currently competing in Algeria chose to take part in events in London. The consequences of aligning with CONIFA ahead of the tournament were substantial for their football association president Aksel Bellabacci.

Bellabaci was arrested and held for questioning for 15 hours by Algerian authorities when the team's participation in London was announced, while some players' families were threatened, too, and forced to swear that their relatives were not members of the independence pushing MAK.

Team manager Lyes Innemai wasn't held for quite as long as Bellbacci, but also had serious issues in the build-up. "I was arrested, and they were blackmailing the players and their families," Innemai explained in London. "We have many players who didn't come because of those threats. The Algerian government still tries to block us and keep everything inside."

It's relatively unusual for Kabylia to be represented in a substantial way outside of the borders of their own disputed territory. Around 5-6 million people in Algeria consider themselves Kabyles, with another one million in France of the same background. They date back to at least the 18th century as an independence movement, and show no signs of calming.

"We are not Algerian, but most of all we're not Arabic," Immemai tells me, perhaps unsurprisingly. "Algeria is afraid of Kabylian independence. We're not afraid of them."

Matchday 4: the arrival of the sharp end.

Ahead of their quarter final, hosts Barawa had already offered to drop into the lower tier of the latter stages of the competition. While CONIFA had accepted circumstances surrounding Mohamed Bettamer's appearance and Ellan Vannin's withdrawal, the integrity of the tournament they were hosting was their primary concern.

In truth, the Somali diaspora side were not in good shape: with the tournament held at the heart of Ramadan, daytime matches didn't allow the players to prepare well. They'd never fully recovered the form of their opening group game, which took place over sunset, which allowed the players to be handed dates midway through the game to try and gather energy to keep going. Now, players were missing for work, too.

Hosted largely during the daytime on a quiet Tuesday, the quarter finals were amongst the worst attended games of the competition. I stood almost alone on Sutton's terraces, watching games with one eye and discussing Cypriot politics with a couple of local pensioners, as my four-year-old spent a determined two hours constructing a character from the Avengers out of Lego.

CONIFA might not claim glamour - it's more about grit, and beating the odds - but there are definitely ebbs and flows in the levels of interest. With the competitors in the quarter finals not confirmed until less than 48 hours before they kicked off, there was also little room for planning from those dedicated to particular sides. The whole thing was surreal; like a fiercely competitive non-league game, but with national anthems, and a handful of deeply involved and extremely passionate fans.

The quarter finals had always been Barawa's target, and they'd come up against a brick wall in high-flying Northern Cyprus. Barawa 'keeper Calvin King is a chunky but athletic type, a fine shot-stopper who is under incessant pressure throughout and makes a couple of early, vital saves, though he also looks vulnerable to crosses and pacey through balls.

In truth, Barawa look exhausted from the off, having turned out in Gander Green Lane with a near-empty subs bench and little in the way of fluid attack. The controversial Bettamer is again their best player, but Billy Mehmet and the young, swift forward line built around him are very much in charge.

Critically, Omar Sufi is sent from the pitch with a green card just before half time, and with Barawa's lack of options on the bench, the dam was about to break. Shortly afterwards, Ugur Naci Gok makes hay from one of the many forays into the Barawa box, and slams the ball home off the back of a Mehmet finish that had been palmed away by King. The 1-0 half time lead is nothing close to reflective of the level of Northern Cyprus' dominance.

They were to get their just rewards in the second half, with Mehmet the chief creator as Gok and Halil Turan add to the scoring. Turan's goal is the best of the set, though by the time he blasts in off the crossbar, Barawa are clearly dead on their feet, and being simply shredded by their impressive opposition.

The final score is 8-0 - the third time such a scoreline has popped up in the course of the tournament, and a true statement of intent for a rampant Northern Cypriot side. The hosts were gone, and there is a slight feeling that their hearts hadn't really been in the game in the first place.

A key question came out of the game for the livid, despatched Ellan Vannin side, who were rumoured to have gone as far as to travel to the game in the hope of being told at late notice that they'd be allowed to play in Barawa's place. Ellan Vannin had hoped to be serious title contenders. Though they hoped to have Barawa's place, the result suggested they weren't up to the mark anyway. If you the Manx were really contenders, how did they manage to lose to a team their rivals just dispatched 8-0?

The second game in Sutton, fortunately, is a far more competitive affair, and serves to highlight the true threat carried by Ukrainian/ Hungarian side Karpatalya. In a contrast of styles,

Karpatalya play composed, possession football, while their north-American opposition Cascadia go for punchy counter-attacks, flying rapidly down the wing, as well as being physically imposing on the ball.

Karpatalya, in the red white and green of their Hungarian ethnicity, rather than their change strip of yellow and blue (a nod to the Ukraine), look marginally more efficient and fluid than their cobbled-together but capable opponents.

Californian winger Max Oldham stands out for the North Americans, a powerful right winger playing with English non-league side Corinthian Casuals. He forms a powerful partnership for Cascadia with Nykøbing FC's Canadian midfield man Jordan Wilson, who plays in the Danish second tier.

There's not a lot of decisive-feeling action in the first half, though a couple of chances for Cascadia do shine through. Josh Doughty bundles over a cross he struggled to fully control early on for Cascadia, and Bela Fejer bundled a finish from Patrick Wilson behind as the west coast side had slightly the better of the first 45 minutes.

Karpatalya are young, fit and used to playing together, however, and explode into life in the second half. György Toma gets the Hungarian side off to a strong start, as he calmly strokes the ball into the corner after a save from Will Marment in the Cascadia goal. The team in red take full control when a weaving run from Robert Molnar lands at the feet of Roland Takacs, who has an easy job tapping in.

The two goals force Cascadia back out of their shell, and half-time substitute Hamza Haddadi breaks through the Karpatalya backline as they grow into the game. His goal, with ten minutes remaining, beats Fejer with a sharp finish and prompts a period of frantic Cascadia pressure.

It isn't to be for Cascadia, though. The contest is put to bed when Karpatalya break forward with three minutes left and are awarded a pretty cheap penalty for a tackle on Zsolt Gajdos, which the midfield man puts away himself.

The Ukrainian side - made up entirely of players based back in their native Hungary, though many were born in the Ukraine - have been a creeping force in the tournament. The last-minute call ups have come out of a strong group, and their relatively comfortable dismissal of strong North American opposition was starting to make people sit up and take notice: were Karpatalya, a rank underdog, better than anyone had realised?

After the game, I think back to a conversation I'd had on the train home from the opening evening's festivities, with CONIFA press officer and Guardian writer Kieran Pender. On hearing of Karpatalya's draw with Northern Cyprus through Twitter, Pender had called the result "quite a turn up," and looked genuinely stunned that the Cypriots hadn't come out on top. That same Karpatalya side were now impressively powering into the final four.

Meanwhile, over in the tournament's most far-flung venue, Bracknell, a powerful looking Padania side are facing their first real challenge of the tournament, having qualified from their group with a game to spare. The northerners face 2016 finalists Panjab, with Padania switching into a Celtic-like green and white hooped strip, and Panjab into their changed blue colours.

A tense and physical match is all about trying to extract the most form tiny chances early on: Panjab threaten from set-pieces and down the wings, while Padania prefer to get the ball on the ground and try and pass through their opponents with Italian flair, though it's to little avail early on.

Pakistan international goalkeeper Yousuf Butt twice stops the Italians towards the end of the half, with Giacomo Innocenti having the best chance as he breaks at pace from the halfway line, only to see his shot closed down by Butt when he should have done better.

There was something effortlessly fluid about the Italians, though. They focus on single-touch passing and pacey manoeuvres, something Panjab clearly struggle with, and while they're not always lethally effective, the look like a really high-class side.

There's a little controversy after the break as Aaron Minhas clears a ball from behind 'keeper Butt for Panjab, as the Italians claim the ball had crossed the line. Still more controversy hits when a soft looking penalty is given for a challenge on the Italian's main man Marius Stankevičius, awarded straight from a corner. Innocenti puts it away to put Padania in front, just reward, perhaps, for the goal they'd just been denied.

A period of Panjab pressure ensues, heightened by an aggressive tension around the contest, and the Asian side look close to grabbing an equaliser through a number of aerial attacks before Padania deliver the sucker punch. Innocenti is the man doing the damage again. He breaks from his own penalty area and plays in Nicolo Pavan, taking goalkeeper Butt out of contention at the same time, for a 90th minute tap in.

Padania had played the better football, but Panjab's traveling support are aggrieved, and not without reason: the penalty, in particular, looked harsh. Innocenti, a former Genoa youth player who's been kicking around the second, third and fourth tiers of Italian football in recent years, is starting to stand out as one of the tournament's star men.

The final quarter final in Bromley pitches Szekely Land against Western Armenia, a game that is heavily weighted in Szekely Land's favour from very early on.

Inside ten minutes, Raffi Kaya brings down Arthur Gyorgyi, and as clearly the last line of the Armenian defence, Kaya, a French-Armenian making his living in the fourth tier of French football, is sent from the pitch.

After Tanko Zsolt slid home the opener for Szekely Land from a looped through ball, the Armenians implode, with their coach sent from the pitchside after an altercation with a fan. Former Hungarian international Csaba Csizmadia adds a second for Szekely Land, before Armenia are reduced to nine for abusive language towards the referee.

From there on it's pretty plain sailing for Szekely Land, with Western Armenia gifting them one of their later goals through a shocking back pass as they stroll into the semi-finals with a 4-0 win. The vociferous Hungarian support is calmed somewhat by the action

127

being midweek, but those who do turn out waving the tricolour or Szekely Land's blue and yellow get a personal thanks from the triumphant Szkelers.

The match had been unusually bad-tempered, the only one at the tournament that stood out as being played in a less than positive spirit. The result, though, was the right one.

Outside what's now the main top-tier competition, a battle for the minor places was taking place without the departed Ellan Vannin. Tibet were awarded an automatic 3-0 win against the Manx side, though they took to the field in a hastily arranged friendly against a local Turkish side in Bromley instead, and were beaten 4-0, with a hat trick from Sporting Bengal's Hassan Nalbant.

Abkhazia had come out and shown what could have been if they hadn't been the losers in a tough group, demolishing the Tamils 6-0 with five second half goals at Aveley FC's tiny Parkside ground, while United Koreans In Japan - the competitions lowest scorers ahead of the game - found their range to put away a lacklustre Tuvalu side 5-0, with the ball hitting the net three times in the opening 23 minutes.

The tightest game came in Enfield, where both sides had goals disallowed for offside as Matabeleland and Kabylia proved extremely closely matched. Ultimately the North Africans overcame the East Africans with a sudden death penalty win.

The quarter finals, in truth, were highlighting the disparity in CONIFA's draw. Those progressing to the semi-finals all came from the same two groups. Northern Cyprus and Karaptalya had put out the holders Abkhazia in group C. Padania and Szekely Land had comfortably controlled Group B. The semi-final results suggested those two groups had been operating on very different levels to the other two, with all four competitors from groups A and D pushed aside.

Matchday 4, Tuesday June 5, 2018

Quarter Final:

Barawa 0-8 Northern Cyprus
Padania 2-0 Panjab
Karpatalya 3-1 Cascadia
Western Armenia 0-4 Szekely Land

Placement rounds (positions 9-16):

Tibet - walkover (officially 3-0, vs Ellan Vannin)
Matabeleland 0-0 Kabylia (Kabylia win 4-3 on penalties)
Abkhazia 6-0 Tamil Eelam
United Koreans In Japan 5-0 Tuvalu

An Aside: A Few CONIFA Questions You Might Want Answered

Does CONIFA work as a route to international football?

I think it's important to say, first, that not every country involved in CONIFA is looking to get involved in more conventional international football, though some certainly are. There is a strong history over years, though, of international football teams starting out as unofficial entities. These range from Nigeria (who can trace their history to 'Nigeria UK Tourists', an unofficial side that toured the UK in 1949), to an unofficial touring Indian team that travelled Australia, Japan, Indonesia and Thailand in the early 1930s, before the establishment of an official national team in the late 40s.

It remains to be seen whether sides like Tuvalu will gain genuine international recognition in the coming years. They are a bit of an exception in terms of the status of any progress with FIFA for CONIFA sides, alongside 'neighbours' Kiribati. Under current FIFA rules, most of the sides involved in CONIFA would have to become countries in the political sense to have any real chance of qualifying for more mainstream internationals. That said, CONIFA did have links with Gibraltar and Kosovo before the pair won UEFA recognition over the last few years, so such changes are not unheard of.

Non-FIFA football has also connected with the Faroe Islands, Monaco and Palestine, sides with really strong claims to nationhood over the years, with the Faroe Islands and Palestine going on to gain more formal recognition. CONIFA can be a stepping stone, though many sides don't see it that way, and are there more in order to represent their identity.

Why does access to this form of international football matter?

Playing for your country is the highest honour a sports person can attain, and in short, to CONIFA competitors, the entity they represent is in many cases what they see as being their nation. Some CONIFA sides have players that have already gone to the highest level for other countries. Ahn Yong-Hak played for North Korea and United Koreans In Japan, and Marius Stankevičius captained Lithuania and turned out for Padania.

It's at the other extreme where these things become important. You might argue that there's no need for a side where a player can go on to represent another nation (I'd disagree, but there's an argument to be had), but few would argue that, for example, Northern Cypriot players, Tuvaluan players or Tibetan players deserve the chance to represent their country. It's unlikely a Tibetan will represent China or India anytime soon, or a Northern Cypriot will break into the Cyprus side. These sides are the only way many of these players will ever get such an opportunity to represent any country. If, as a sportsman, you can't dream of the very heights of the international game, what's left to dream of?

How good are the CONIFA sides?

The honest answer is it's very difficult to say, but I'll give it a shot. Some of them are really quite poor by any real standard. While the likes of Tuvalu, Tibet and Matabeleland are certainly better than you'd expect given the difficulties they've faced in getting to CONIFA in London, you'd have to drop a long way down the league pyramid in England, for example, to find a team they'd be competitive against. They'd probably slide in somewhere in the ninth or tenth tier.

The better sides in the tournament, however are serious outfits, and while they might suffer the lack of coherence that often comes with any type of international football (they simply don't spend enough time playing together), I personally felt the sides in the last four might have survived an English League one season without going down. But perhaps I'm being optimistic.

Panjab and Barawa: Vastly Differing Diaspora Sides

Panjab - Founded: 2014 Record Win: 9-1 v Alderney Record Loss: 8-1 v Ellan Vannin Distance from London (side's spiritual home): 3928 miles (6322 kms) Home Capital: Amritsar, India Player Pool Playing In: England, Denmark, Germany CONIFA Ranking: 1

Barawa - Founded: 2015 Record Win: 4-0 v Tamil Eelam Record Loss: 8-0 v Northern Cyprus Distance from London (side's spiritual home): 4323 miles (6957 kms) Home Capital: Barawa, Somalia Player Pool Playing In: England CONIFA Ranking: 11

In their book, 'Why England Lose', Simon Kuper and Stefan Szymanski apply various statistical techniques to footballing conundrums. They use a vast amount of data to explore issues like whether England overachieve or underachieve at international tournaments (even prior to the 2018 World Cup, they slightly overachieve), the statistically best way to bring in more fans to a club (not to improve the team, it turns out, but to improve the stadium), and what contributes to a successful national team (the country's overall experience, GDP, and population are the key factors). They also touch upon racism.

The book's statistical approach to tackling whether racism is prevalent in English football is based on whether teams with similar wage bills (the best measure of a side's likely success - it accounts for over 90% of league position) perform better if they contain more black players. The logic, of course, is that if such a correlation exists with any strength, it would be heavily indicative of discrimination: if black players systematically achieve more whilst being paid less, it follows that they are discriminated against.

Their data, you'll be pleased to hear, shows such discrimination was once strongly present, but that it essentially ceased to exist in the 90s. Yes, that is depressingly late, but it was the footnote attached to that statistic that interested me more: British Asians lack of success in professional football.

Back when Kuper and Szymanski's statistics began, almost 90% of black players playing for English clubs were born in the UK. They were typically the children of fairly recent immigrants, present in the UK no more than a couple of generations. British Asians, however, outnumber British blacks substantially.

Lots of fairly serious football fans would struggle to name a professional British Asian player (Michael Chopra, who played up front for Newcastle, Sunderland and Cardiff, and Aston Villa's Neil Taylor, a Welsh international with an Indian mother, are a couple of standouts). In the 2008/2009 season, the book tells us, there were only seven British Asian professionals in all of English football. There hasn't been a full England international of notable Asian heritage since the 1930s.

If you want to take it to a real extreme, there's even an argument to be made, in fact, that the 2002 movie 'Bend It Like Beckham' has had more cultural impact than any Asian-British footballer, right up until today. The film portrays the journey of a Panjabi-British girl, Jesminder Bhamra (Parminder Nagra), who falls in love with the game against her parents' wishes. She gets involved with a local team in Hounslow, shows her ability, finds herself critical to their chances of success, and (spoiler alert) ultimately scores a critical free-kick reminiscent of Mr Beckham himself and wins a scholarship abroad.

The comparison might sound flippant, but even the English FA seem to have given up on British-Asian achievement in high-end football. In 2017, the BBC worked out that British Asians make up only ten of the 3000 professional footballers in the country. Given 7% of the population of England is Asian, even allowing for those who choose to play their international football for other countries (there are a handful of Pakistani internationals in the British lower tiers), there should be a British Asian in the majority of England squads, all things being equal.

The English Football Association have held meetings on the issue as recently as 2014, but admitted later that year, through then chairman Greg Dyke, that attempts to improve participation had failed, despite holding cross-country forums with the Asian community.

"It's clear that however well-intentioned the FA and other football bodies have been in the past... change hasn't materialised," Dyke said, adding that he feels. "The passion has not quite translated."

"From my own experiences in club football, I know the appetite is there for Asians to be involved in the game at all levels," he said.

"Yet only a handful of players have made the professional playing ranks over the past two decades. Players like Zesh Rehman, Harpal Singh, Michael Chopra, Adil Nabi and Permi Jhooti have been the exception rather than the rule."

Panjab, then, have plenty of reason to push themselves forward locally. They also have a positive message: Panjab represent the diaspora of an area of West India and East Pakistan, crossing the border. That area is now in a state of seemingly permanent near-conflict, yet the Panjabi side embrace both sides of the conflict, making them something of a throwback to the days before India and Pakistan's segregation along religious lines.

The area is one of the oldest inhabited regions in the world, a place that's changed hands countless times over the years, impacted by Muslim and Sikh Empires and British imperialism in particular.

The founder of Sikhism, Guru Nanak, was from this part of the world, and a gloriously peaceful temple, the Golden Temple of Amritsar, is still widely seen as the religion's most holy location. The gold-plated building sits in the heart of a serene lake, used for bathing by the devout. In line with Sikh religious beliefs, even today anyone who arrives at the temple will be fed, watered, and offered a bed for the night without payment.

The town of Shimla, also in the region, was a central seat of British power in north India, in part because its weather was so much more comfortable for the British rulers. Amritsar, the region's Sikh

135

heart, suffered its most severe colonial consequences in April 1919, when a walled garden in the city became the site of a massacre of at least 379 - and possibly thousands - as troops reacted to what they perceived as an Indian nationalist meeting by blocking the exits and firing on the crowd for a full ten minutes. The moment was a key turning point in the ending of British control in the country.

That was only for starters. To say that the split into India and Pakistan had a profound and horrifying impact when Hindustan was partitioned is a massive understatement. Estimates put the post-division death toll at between 200,000 and two million. Very few Muslims survive in modern day India, and very few Hindus in modern day Pakistan. The clashes, largely fought along religious lines, were horrifying and echo in Indian and Pakistani politics today.

The modern-day footballing incarnation of the Panjab's peaceful side, which somehow sweeps aside that history, was formed by Harpreet Singh, a Sikh activist born in the UK. Singh claims his side represent the largest population of any side at CONIFA, with most estimates putting the global Punjabi population at over 100 million people.

Panjab aren't the first side to try and represent the Punjabi community: a Kent tenth-tier club playing in the English league system, Punjab FC, are dedicated to promoting south Asian soccer locally in the south east, but Panjab are certainly the biggest attempt so far.

At CONIFA, the Panjabi side, like Northern Cyprus in Enfield, were granted the chance to connect with a strong local community, and played their group matches to the west of London, in a traditional Panjabi hot spot, Slough. They wowed the passionate local crowd with an opening 8-0 thrashing of Kabylia, before edging out of a tight group to reach the last eight.

"The Panjabi FA knew about the venue, Slough, but held it back to make a big announcement to get the Panjabi community in Slough excited about it," JD Singh, a Panjabi supporter and live-match commentator told us at one of the games. "The weekend games had a huge turn-out, with all the traditional drums out. It's had a great impact on our tournament."

"There's a lot of enthusiasm for this. Panjab don't have the problems that other teams have with getting the best players who are eligible to come and play. I think we've selected pretty much the best squad that was available to us for this tournament. They've had no problem getting players, and they'll have no problem attracting players in the future."

Perhaps the best symbol of the Panjabi side, drawn from both Indian and Pakistan, but largely from the Sikh community, is that passionate founder of the Panjab FA, Harpreet Singh. Singh is a serious, intense man who believes almost single-mindedly in what he's doing, and declared himself 'extremely disappointed' when the number-one ranked side failed to progress beyond the quarterfinal in London.

When the Panjabi anthem plays, Singh stands tall at the front of the crowd in his turban and bellows the anthem-closing war cry out onto the pitch at the top of his voice. He's so vocal in doing so, at one game a supporter mistook his impassioned cry for an anti-CONIFA protest.

"This has given an opportunity to a lot of players, mostly playing at the tenth, eleventh of twelfth tiers of English football, who perhaps had never really considered international football as an option. There are about two million British Panjabis. We might well see a lot of people exploring their Panjabi heritage because of this competition." JD Singh explains.

Those origins are quite distinct and hard to fathom in a modern context. "We're talking about pre-partition days," Singh explains, "Before India and Pakistan existed. Before that it was all Hindustan. Funnily enough, the village that my family originally come from… when they left India it was part of India. Now it's part of Pakistan."

"It's an unusual one. I claim my Indian heritage, and a large number of my Panjabi friends would claim their Indian heritage, but a lot of the villages we actually come from are now in Pakistan, not

India. It's an anomaly of geography that our country was split up so arbitrarily in the forties."

"They split our Holy land deep straight down the middle," he continues. "We've kind of had to play politics with both sides just to be able to exist. Both countries were drawn up for religious reasons, but the minor religions in India, the Buddhists, the Jains, the Dalits, the Sikhs have very much fallen by the wayside in the last 60 years."

"The current government in India, without meaning to be controversial, is very much a Brahmin Hindu style government, where if you're born to the right caste and the right family, you're ok. If not, tough luck. This gives an opportunity for people who feel a little bit separated from their cultural identity to be able to identify themselves. Football is a universal language that traverses politics, sexuality, language, all that," Singh says, exploring the strength of the team he's come to love.

"If football is the way we can help some of the more disparate parts of our society connect with their homeland, let football be the language that we speak. It works well within the team, as well. Panjab's goalkeeper is Pakistan's first choice international goalkeeper. You might assume there are divisions between states, but there aren't."

"We'd have to be the poster boys for integration when it comes to this competition. Hindus, Muslims and Sikhs have been fighting each other for years, but when it comes to this competition, we all get on board. It doesn't matter. All that matters is the yellow shirt that we're playing in."

Panjab don't shy away from the lack of success for Asian footballers in the UK. In fact, trials for Aran Basi, a former Leeds United school boy, and two others from the 2016 Panjabi squad with Notts County after the tournament concluded helped drive interest in the team, and confirmed that it's making progress, though none of the three won deals at the league two club.

"We just want a British Asian to break through, whether he's Sikh, Hindu, Muslim of whatever, it doesn't matter," Singh explains. "There was a cultural evolution that happened in the game forty years ago with players that came over from the West Indies and players with African heritage. British Asians have only really been here for 40 odd years in total."

"We need to have our moment, our one, and to tell you the truth, if he makes it under the banner of being a British Asian, it will break the walls down for an awful lot of players."

When it comes to kick off, Harpreet Singh bellows the rallying call of Guru Gobind Singhg, a call dating back to 1699. Gobind Singhg was the 10th Sikh guru, responsible for the formation of Sikhism of its modern-day form, and stood at the head of a notorious army. It was said did not fear death. The team take to the pitch in honour of ancient beliefs and a country that no longer exists.

It doesn't really go quite to plan: while they've been passionately backed and engaged heavily with the community in Slough, with their tournament over, Panjab aren't happy.

"It's not really good enough to go from second to a best possible finish of fifth," Harpreet Singh says after his side are knocked out by Italians Padania in the quarter finals. Panjab might be ranked number one in CONIFA going into the tournament, but they are made up mainly of players from the depths of the English league system. On paper, they look outclassed.

That said, they had led the 2016 CONIFA World Cup final right up until the 88th minute, before losing to hosts Abkhazia on sudden death penalties. In an odd bit of trivia around the team, Sunderland born Amar Purewal's goal for Panjab in that game makes him the first British man to score in a world-level senior final since Geoff Hurst in 1966. Panjab have, traditionally, been serious competitors on this level.

"They have to step up," Singh argues. It's hard not to admire the lofty goals, but on paper, against ever-improving CONIFA opponents, Panjab have found their level.

Barawa's perspective is entirely different. Their side is not so much an opportunity to represent people who otherwise wouldn't have such a noticeable voice. It's more a tribute.

Barawa didn't even exist when the previous global edition of CONIFA was held in 2016 in Abkhazia, and technically represent a small town of 32,000 people, though the reality actually sees the squad take on members from places as far afield as Jamaica.

In the early days, the aim had been simply to bring the community together, and perhaps send a little bit of money back to their struggling homeland after raising it through their games. That turned out to be quite misguided: running the team cost quite a substantial amount of money; more so when they became one of those responsible for putting together the London tournament from a logistical perspective.

There might not be money, but there is awareness. Even before the tournament got underway in London, the team were making noises about how they hoped to have an influence back in Somalia, improving football access and infrastructure following the Barawa stadium attack.

"We want to go home, host a league, and have players playing at a good standard," captain Omar Sufi said ahead of the tournament. I want to give them the opportunity to come and play for Barawa. That's definitely a long-term aim."

"The first time we played the Tamil boys, we lost 5-0, which for me was a bit embarrassing. Now we're playing them again in front of the whole media, the public, I just can't wait." Barawa want on to win that opening game 4-0.

The Semi Finals: An Intense Road to Glory

Both semi-finals are scheduled back to back at Carshalton United, a Subbuteo pitch of a place a brisk trek from the nearest train station, where CONIFA seems to have taken off in a big way.

The roads to the stadium are packed with fans waving their colours, and while the crowds inside are modest for the first contest, it seems almost everyone in the stadium had engaged with the competition and passions run high.

Behind the Padanian bench, an Italian fan sits atop the low fence and belts out songs all game long, like he's leading the choir on the terraces of Milan or Lazio, minus the loudspeaker.

In breaks in play, he chats to the coaching staff, trying to convince the Padania manager to share his half-full glass of white wine (Italian, naturally). A Vice journalist drops over to speak to him, while half a dozen Turkish Cypriots get increasingly riled by his mocking of their players.

It turns out the most vocal fan in the stadium isn't even from Padania. "I'm Sicilian," he explains. The south Italian region would, typically, be politically against the concept of Padania. "I just miss football, and this is the only Italian team at a World Cup this summer. That hurts, you know? They're Italian. That's enough, I'll follow them."

It's not just the football that's appealed to a few spectators: as well as no standing areas, no option to have a beer while you watch the game is a commonly complaint levelled at the upper echelons of English football. Chugging beers between the burger stalls in the depths of high-end football stadiums has become a footballing halftime rite of passage, but unrestricted by football's conventional rules, plenty are supping pints at pitch side as the bigger games get underway.

Padania and Northern Cyprus is a real clash of the titans when it comes to non-FIFA internationals. Padania have taken numerous titles over the years, while Northern Cyprus were totally unbeaten in non-FIFA competition for years after they started out, and match the Italians in their professionalism. The minor contests are over: both these sides are clearly here to win, and have plenty of history to build on, too. Padania beat Northern Cyprus in the 2017 CONIFA European Football Cup final in the Cypriots' backyard, taking the title 4-2 on penalties.

The quality is an immediate step up. Northern Cyprus twice get in on Padania's goal in the early stages, but got barged off the ball for the first, before lofting a second finish just over the crossbar.

A back-post header for Mehmet saw a third big chance for the Cypriots, but the ball was palmed around the post, to arguments that it may have crossed the line. They were punished for their profligacy as Riccardo Ravasi finished off a flowing break from the back, instigated by key man Marius Stankevicius, who was proving a rock of passing flair in the backline.

Billy Mehmet hit back just five minutes later, finally getting the better of a solid Padania defence and rewarding Northern Cyprus' strong showing by using his strength near the penalty spot to turn and slide the ball into the far corner.

It became clear at that moment that much of the crowd were behind Northern Cyprus. While the Padania goal was greeted with modest applause and a leap onto the barrier by the rowdy man with his bottle of white, the Northern Cypriot goal was met with genuine enthusiasm, hundreds of fans leaping to their feet and punching the air.

The Padanians, though, are nothing if not efficient. Stankevicius was key to a couple more attacks, his long, looping balls seemingly able to find anyone on the pitch at any time. He played into the build-up of Nicolo Pavan's slotted goal, worked wide on the left. Padania went in at the break with a 2-1 lead in what had been an entertaining contest.

Most of the key moments of the second half came at the Padania, end, as the Northern Cyprus drive for the final stepped up. They were threatened consistently on the break, but could have scored several times if not for last-gasp defensive efforts from the despairing - but still leading - men in hooped green and white.

Mehmet had a chance he probably should have scored with a free header at the far post. Padania scrambled a couple of strong chances from their goal mouth, and eventually the breakthrough came. It was Halil Turan who ultimately headed an equaliser into the Padania goal, after Mehmet's header from a corner was punched unconvincingly clear by Padania goalkeeper Marco Murriero.

The 80th minute equaliser prompted emphatic scenes in the stands with the entire squad gathering around Turan on the touchline. They were to go one better: Padania swung a free kick over the bar through Stankevicius, before Turan broke to play in Mehmet six yards out, and he slammed an 84th minute winner into Murriero's goal, evoking another wild celebration.

The slight underdogs had Padania on the ropes, and had three more solid chances, including a breakaway one-on-one with Murriero - lifted straight into his hands - before things were finally over. As they held the ball in the corner, frustration got the better of the experienced Stankevicius, whose slap at a Cypriot forward saw him dismissed.

Northern Cyprus' win prompted chaos: a pitch invasion, dancing in the stands, and the realisation that the Turkish-Cypriot community would be turning out in force for the final, which would be hosted in Turkish-heavy Enfield.

The party goes on into the car park, the songs of the players and their fans echoing over the stand from near the team buses as players warm up for the second semi-final, played directly afterwards. Padania had taken the CONIFA European title away from Northern Cyprus in their own backyard a year earlier. The team in red and their substantial backing were savouring their revenge.

Ahead of the second semi-final, the Carshalton crowds grow substantially as punters drift in for the post-work kick off. The Hungarian fans - in particular those backing Szekely Land - have been a consistently strong feature of the tournament, rabid and playful in their approach to games, which are treated as a kind of gathering point for the London Hungarian community.

There's also an odd connection emerging with a couple of London football clubs. Karpatalya seem popular with the Carshalton Athletic fans. Spurs fans had come out in numbers to sing songs that are half about Tottenham, and half about Szekely Land.

The game seemed to be technical ability vs. physical stature, with the young, proficient Karpatalya side slick on the floor and nicely set up, while Szekely Land played a more aggressive, thundering game.

Karpatalya had claimed the Hungarian colours for the day, while pale blue Szekely Land got the better of the opening minute, threatening down both wings as they attempted to launch the ball to big, chunky strikers.

Karpatalya grew into the game, though, and started to cause plenty of hassle, first stealing the ball from the Szekely 'keeper, only to be denied at the last, and then seeing a well-worked attack deflected wide of the mark when it looked likely to be heading in.

It's a moment of pure class from midfielder Yuriy Toma that eventually breaks the deadlock. The Cigánd SE man, who plays in the Hungarian second tier, skipped through three or four Szekely midfielders, straight through the middle of the pack, and then finished past Adrian Horvát in the Szekely goal.

Almost immediately, Mark Clattenburg awarded a penalty at the other end, against Karpatalya goalkeeper Béla Fejér, who caught a breaking striker as he tried to lob him from close range. Fejér redeems himself immediately in stopping the spot kick, and Karpatalya went in with a 1-0 lead.

Most of the Hungarians in the crowd were behind Szekely Land, but their passion was directed a little differently this time. With flags draped around the stadium, they light their flairs and chant their songs, but most of them are purely Hungarian love-ins, the chants seemingly directed in appreciation of both sides. The locals were getting drawn into the passion, and early in the second half, a flood of fans made their way into one corner of the stadium, where much of the noise was coming from, to get involved.

Outsiders Karpatalya, though, were starting to put their foot down, despite Fejér having regularly work to do himself. It was Toma who made the breakthrough again after 56 minutes, though the goal was largely thanks to a goalkeeping error, with Horvát hitting a swerving shop straight down the 'keepers throat, only to see it parried into the net.

From there, Szekely Land were forced into a far more attacking set up. Former Hungarian international centre back Csaba Csizmadia was growing into the game, directing play from the back, and threading neat through balls and arching deep crosses into his attacking players.

Szekely Land missed a procession of good chances, but were undone once again by the charging Toma. He was hacked down on the break, but passed on the opportunity to go for his hat trick, handing the ball to Gergő Gyürki, who calmly rolled it into the bottom right hand corner.

Oddly, at 3-0 down and with only 15 minutes remaining, Szekely Land finally stepped up to the plate. Fejér made another point blank save in a goalmouth scramble. Csizmadia finally beat Fejér a minute later, and after Szekely Land sprinted back to the half way line, Barna Bajkó found the ball at his feet 25 yards out and smashed it straight into the corner of the Karpatalya goal.

Suddenly a dead rubber was alive again, with 12 minutes still remaining and the momentum very much with the Szekely side. They fashioned a series of chances, but it wasn't to be: instead Karpatalya turned down the game-killing corner flag play a minute into injury time, and caught Szekely Land out by playing in Csaba Peres, who stroked home and put Karpatalya through.

The 4-2 result came against expectations, with the Karpatalya side having fallen short of qualifying for the tournament at the first attempt. The late call up were now in the final. The result also ensured Karpatalya and Northern Cyprus would face off again in the finale, after drawing 1-1 in the group stage.

The two semi-finals had been the outstanding games of the tournament, setting CONIFA on fire after a disappointing set of quarterfinals. With 11 goals between them and a whole lot of passion, this was CONIFA at its very, very best.

Padania - the elephant in the room?

Founded: 1998 *Record Win:* 20-0 v *Darfur* *Record Loss:* 2-0 v *Ausonia* *Distance Travelled to London:* 664 miles (1068 kms) *Home Capital:* Po Valley, Italy *Player Pool Playing In:* Italy, USA *CONIFA Ranking:* 2

In 2015, a team called Padania, from Northern Italy, arrived into CONIFA's world. Having been supported by extreme right-wing party Lega Nord during their time playing under the NF Board, Padania were certain to be a cause of some controversy, and a challenge to the concept of CONIFA's political neutrality.

Lega Nord are a populist, regionalist party in Northern Italy who, at times, have campaigned heavily on North Italian separatism. They currently sit at the right-wing of the Italian political spectrum, their previous acts include the election of an unofficial Padanian parliament, the symbolic pouring of water from the Po River into the sea at Venice as an act of 'forming a nation', and close affiliations with France's National Front. To say Lega Nord are a controversial subject in Italy is something of an understatement.

Padania were, in their early days, an overtly political and starkly right-wing team, and while not endorsing their view, NF Board were okay with that. After all, their other teams included Sealand, a 'country' without enough people living in to actually form a football team (they did anyway, somehow), so omitting a genuine entity, if one some might turn their noses up at, probably seemed a bit daft. CONIFA were less accepting. Padania were rejected, at least initially, and told to come back minus the overt political connections to the Lega Nord, via a heavy restructuring, if they wanted to play.

"You know Italians, they always think they play the best and most beautiful football," CONIFA CEO Per-Anders Blind jokes. "They sit on pedestals."

The Padanians are traditionally the richest people of Italy, and at the other end of the social spectrum fall the Romani gypsies. The two played in the 2015 CONIFA European Cup, and after a tight 3-2 victory for Padania, the symbolic hug between the players at full time remains one of Blind's favourite CONIFA memories. "They showed respect on the pitch and became friends. Knowing the background, that gave me goose bumps," he recalls.

It's fair to say, given the regional history, that nobody wants a European team with overt links to fascism given airtime. It's also fair to say that some elements of Italian football have done a poor job of distancing themselves from hard right politics, so much so that there's an entire book out there on the subject, 'Football, Fascism and Fandom: The Ultras of Italian Football'. Lazio, from Rome, are particularly notorious.

Padania, though, have done their utmost to distance themselves from any such thoughts, and the inclusion of Lithuanian long-time resident Stankevicius is perhaps a good example of the team's more 'open' approach than its political ancestry might suggest.

In fact, on investigation, Padania football's link to Lega Nord is really quite a paper one: Padanians are generally more in favour of the ideal of a more federalist Italy than they are of a free Padania anyway, with recent polls showing no more than 20% in support of the idea of splitting from Italy entirely.

I try to ask a couple of Padania fans and players about the connection through the tournament. It's universally, passionately denied: this is simple a representation of a region. If the team's supposed to be a symbol of Italian fascism, they're doing an impressive job of pretending otherwise.

Mid way through the tournament, I was sent an image by Twitter private message showing a CONIFA player with a swastika lightly inked on his arm. It was a barely visible, yet distinct outline, and after careful thought, I've decided not to even mention the team he played for here. It wasn't, however, a Padanian.

Around the Grounds: Day Five Placement Games

Like the closing games of a league season, there's a mixed level of seriousness to the latter placement games at CONIFA. Some play for pride, others see the latter stages as a chance to rotate their squad, giving a first taste of this type of football to those who hadn't made the group games.

They all count, of course, when it comes to rankings, apart from one. Matabeleland are taking their turn to 'play' the departed Ellan Vannin squad (or rather, receive a 3-0 walkover); they actually play fill-in side Chagos Islands at Aveley, and win 1-0 through a headed goal in front of a depleted crowd. The win is irrelevant, but does send Matabeleland through to a play-off for 13th v 14th in the tournament on the final day.

Perhaps wary of the controversy around Barawa's squad earlier in the tournament, Matabeleland finally brought out Grobbelaar in goal now that their game was a friendly, and the 'keeper proved more than capable as he played a half an hour at the start of the game. Being a friendly, in fact, Matabeleland saw a chance to ease their financial concerns, and auctioned two places on the pitch, too. As well as Grobbelaar, the two auction winners and the entire Matabeleland coaching staff all got a run out.

At the top end of the placement games, sides are playing for a top finish of 5th, and Panjab take the chance to take out their frustrations. The south Asian side had high expectations going into the World Football Cup, and a depleted and recently-thrashed Barawa side put up little resistance, with Kamaljit Singh hitting four in a 5-0 Panjab win in Sutton.

Singh had given Panjab an early lead, after which Barawa will point to a key turning point. After less than half an hour, striker Simon Noel went over in the Panjab penalty area under pressure from Pakistan international Yousuf Butt. The referee deemed the fall a dive, and Noel was handed a green card, with Barawa's only available placement the already-injured Omar Sufi.

Barawa hung on at 1-0 until half time, even dominating for a period, but their resistance broke in the second half and Panjab - and Singh in particular - ran wild. I'd spent the game sat next to the heavily-engaged Panjabi commentary team, relaying details onto an online radio station, and found myself utterly caught up in their passion.

In Bromley, meanwhile, Cascadia, were getting better every game, and also hit a glut against Western Armenia, turning the game on its head after they looked overrun in the early stages. Cascadia came out 4-0 winners, with Calum Ferguson grabbing two in a bad-tempered contest.

The Americans were relaxing into the tournament and letting their natural athleticism play out: had they had a little more time together, they'd clearly have been a real contender for the 2018 title.

In the lower half of the draw, Abkhazia were finally showing why they'd been tagged as favourites ahead of the tournament, seeing off the defensively-minded United Koreans In Japan.

The game in Bromley was a mellow affair, with a poor goalkeeping display from the usually reliable Shim Woodae contributing to a 2-0 Abkhazia win, with the Korean side again less than potent in front of goal.

On the other side of the draw, Tibet had a disaster of a second half against Kabylia, having given the Algerians a real early scare. Karma Tsewang was sent off for the Tibetans after the constant threat of Sami Boudia had been rewarded with a goal. That looked to have derailed Tibet's challenge, but they broke through Kalsang Topgyal, their most consistent goal threat, and won a penalty late in the first half. He dispatched it to bring things level.

The man disadvantage could only be overcome for so long, though, as the Tibetans were broken in the second half. They'd conceded a goal just before the break, but continued to attack, showing a certain naivety as they allowed themselves to be opened up at the back. Sami Baudia, a Racing Club de Paris player, hit 4, with the 18-year-old later awarded young player of the tournament for his efforts, winning a chance to train in academies in Spain and Holland.

The game of the day, though, came in Sutton, as Tamil Eelam met Tuvalu. Tuvalu had scored only once in the tournament ahead of the game, but hit the net inside three minutes though Teufaiva Ionatana, only to concede another three minutes later, with Prashanth Ragavan played clear. That Tamil goal was their first of the tournament, and the game wasn't yet ten minutes old.

Most of the action came in the second half, though, after Tuvalu had survived a first half onslaught, including with a penalty save from Katepu Iosua. This was passionate, carefree football, and Tuvalu's free-flowing approach was particularly appetizing.

The Pacific islanders had a penalty of their own saved early in the second half, but took control through Sosene Vailiene, and then set up a tap in for Alopua Petoa to lead three one with fifteen minutes remaining.

That should have been it, but Tamil Eelam piled on the pressure and pulled off the most unlikely of turnarounds. Ragavan completed his hat trick with goals in the 86th and 91st minute, before a 94th minute winner looped over the goalkeeper's head and broke Tuvalu hearts. Tamil Eelam, who had scored only one goal in the entire tournament prior to the final ten minutes of this contest, had hit an unlikely winning trio.

Matchday 5 Results: Thursday June 7, 2018

Semi finals

Northern Cyprus 3-2 Padania
Karpatalya 4-2 Szekely Land

5th to 8th place games
Cascadia 4-0 Western Armenia
Barawa 0-5 Panjab

9th to 12th place games

Abkhazia 2-0 United Koreans In Japan
Tibet 1-8 Kabylia

13th to 16th place games

Tamil Eelam 4-3 Tuvalu
Matabeleland 3-0 Ellan Vannin (walkover)
Matabeleland defeat Chagos Islands 1-0 in replacement friendly contest.

A broader context: how is footballing accessibility in London?

Ubiquitous in their pale pink and dark blue shades, Dulwich Hamlets have quite the 'football hipster', yuppie fan reputation. In niche footballing circles, stories are forever doing the rounds about one of south London's most unusual clubs. They travel to Hamburg and play their German counterparts in Altona '93, drinking in the red light district until the early hours afterwards. At corners, their fans whip out their expensive car keys and jangle them behind the goal, signifying a 'key moment' and earning the ire of traditional football fans throughout the league. Some, they say, come more for the club's craft beer and pop-up food tents than for the game.

Whatever your take on Dulwich Hamlets, there's no question they are one of the best supported sides in sixth tier English football. They were supposed to host at CONIFA, but the club's own difficulties got in the way: their Champion Hill ground was considered so important locally that it was once listed as an asset of community value, but that wasn't enough to prevent it being snapped up by property developers, and listed for redevelopment.

London real estate is extremely valuable, and Hamlet's well-located stadium was set to be a victim. A mass protest from fans got underway, and while some compromises were made by the development company, Meadows Residential, nobody at Hamlets was ever going to agree to the destruction of their stadium.

Instead of playing their games in their own ground, Dulwich Hamlets ground was locked up at the time CONIFA came to London, with the team forced to kick off their 2018/2019 season down the road, in the stadium of their traditional local rivals Tooting & Mitcham.

Hamlets' problems got me wondering how difficult it is to play football in London. Do the fringes of society have access to the game, or is it the preserve of those who can afford to play? The answer seems, on the face of it, obvious: there's a lot of green space in London, and football is hardly an expensive way to pass the time. It turns out it's not quite that simple.

If you wanted a model of a pure, free-market capitalist system, football is probably it. There are twists on that, of course: clubs that should go bankrupt often don't, as fans rally round (you certainly wouldn't see that at a company). Clubs can thrive, to an extent, based on relationships, particularly in the lower tiers, where good links to a strong club with higher level players can make a huge difference in loan signings that can be brought in, and lead to success. Overall, though, the correlation between the total salaries of the players on display and the league position teams finish in is frightening, a stat that's somewhat depressing as a football fan. You could, quite reasonably, argue that things are mostly about money.

Londoner Billy Beckett runs an organisation called 'Terrible Football,' and it's emphatically not about money. In fact, it's designed for those who don't have any, as well as those who don't want to connect with football in its more traditional form. Perhaps they're not very good, or perhaps they don't want the commitment. The idea is simple: games in parks, throughout London, accessible to anyone who wants to get involved. They currently have close to 4000 members.

"Have you always wanted to play football, but are too intimidated to join a local Sunday League team, or don't want to fork out cash for a five-a-side on astroturf?" the ads run. "Fancy a relaxed kick about in the park? Then this group is for you!"

"We want to provide a place for people to play football where nobody is judged and nobody takes it too seriously."

Beckett and his Terrible Football concept - inspired by the running equivalent 'ParkRun' - also get themselves involved in charities like 'Football Beyond Borders'. He has plenty to say about the surprising difficulties some people have in accessing the game.

I sit in a park outside Haringey Borough as Burkett takes me through his project. "It's avowedly terrible. It's got its roots in jumpers for goalpost park football, and we maintain that kind of ethos. It's inclusive, it's all abilities, and mixed gender, and age. It started in 2015 and grew from there. In the summer, games might draw 80 people, so we play six or seven a side, six games simultaneously," he says, talking me through the project with boisterous enthusiasm.

"The diversity of London is really reflected in the games, and also the geographical regions of London," Burkett says. "If you go and play in Bethnal Green, for example, you get a lot of Pakistani and Bangladeshi boys. I like how it reflects the culture. In Bethnal Green right now [during Ramadan], we're playing with these Muslim boys who are in incredibly bad moods. They're playing football, and they haven't eaten. You have these nice funny cultural things that happen."

"It's a nightmare to play on proper pitches in London," Burkett continues. "Land is so valuable, and they often sell it to build a block of flats. That makes pitches more expensive to play on. If you look at Hackney, there are no clubs in Hackney. Not a single club at a higher level than a school team. Hackney has a massive population and a lot of people that are into that kind of thing, but there's not a ground."

"I know groups that have tried to petition the local council to build a ground, but they haven't got the cash. A borough like Hackney not having something like that, being home to over a quarter of a million people, is insanity. The FA have a football community fund that you can apply for grants from, but it's a limited pot. It's not really directed to building grassroots football."

"You see some players, people like Rio Ferdinand and Mark Noble who are genuinely good at giving back. Some West Ham players have put a load of money into building affordable housing for people. There are avenues for doing this kind of stuff, but it's not easy," he continues.

"My experience is this stuff really goes to the poorest in the community, in terms of impacts. Terrible Football has a lot of members, but the most passionate are often the diverse London communities, people who might not have another chance to play football. Especially in London, it's easy to be pushed out."

There should be another motivation behind this, too. Putting aside any sense of altruism or equality for a moment, the England side thrives on players who come from working class backgrounds, very often tied to immigration. Of the 23-man squad that travelled to Russia (and reached a little-anticipated World Cup semi-final), origins could be traced to Jamaica, Ghana, Guyana, Ivory Coast, Portugal, Ireland, Nigeria, the US, and the tiny Caribbean island of St Kitts. If you want an argument for wider inclusion, there's a very easy one: what we already have has been essential to success.

"We are a team with our diversity and youth that represents modern England," head coach Gareth Southgate told ITV. "We are the reflection of a new identity and we hope that people connect with us." The Guardian - as, admittedly, is their wont - pointed this out in detail in an article titled 'What do the World Cup semi-finalists all have in common? Immigration.' Ahead of the semis, they showed that the other three sides involved in the later stages of the World Cup, France, Belgium, and Croatia also had a hefty weighting of immigrants running through their line ups. France, the winners, could trace an astonishing 78% of their squad to immigrant backgrounds elsewhere.

For an English football fan, selfishness and the drive for success alone should be enough to want problems with access blown wide open. But this is our national game. Should we really need alternative motivations and people with the vision of Burkett to push us to let everyone in?

Tibet: The Forbidden Team

Founded: 1994 Record Win: 12-2 v Western Sahara Record Loss: 22-0 v Provence Distance Travelled to London: 3962 miles (6376 kms) Home Capital: Dharamshala, India (via Lhasa, Chinese Occupied Tibet) Player Pool Playing In: India CONIFA Ranking: 13 (and last of the ranked sides)

"It's not just a question of playing football. It's a question of freedom to play football," Michael Nybrandt, then Tibetan football boss, says in 2003 Danish football documentary Det Forbudte Landshold (The Forbidden Team). It's a few days before a planned game against Greenland, and Tibet have been through an arduous process getting there, hurdling barriers at seemingly every turn.

They've appointed Nybrandt, a Danish coach, ahead of their first game outside of India, and held a three-week training camp in the hills to try and forge a team. After the camp, they've had to dismiss a number of players due to the status of their travel papers. Their Danish visas have been held up until the last minute, as their passports are not official documents, but refugee documents with a 'leave to return' stamp renewed by India every two years. Their main training and matchday pitch, in the mountain town of Dharamshala, is also a public road. It's regularly crossed by a procession of people and cows, holding up play as they meander through. Things, it's fair to say, are far from conventional.

It's a miracle that the team ever arrive in Denmark at all, but they do, a week before the game, only to find the political pressure on. In protest, the Chinese are threatening to hit Denmark's export industry - in particular Greenland's shrimp exports - in a major way if the game goes ahead. Even the host ground's owners are thinking of pulling out. A relatively poor-quality game quickly becomes a national political debate in Denmark, covered across the news.

Organiser Michael Nybrant ultimately has to visit the Chinese embassy in Copenhagen and argue the case for his team. He sits and listens to an in-depth spiel about Tibet's status as part of China, but the game is allowed to go ahead.

When the side finally do walk out it's in front of a crowd of over 5,000 in a packed Vanløse Stadium in west Copenhagen, many of whom are waving Tibetan flags. The reception is boisterous. Tibet's first international goal is scored by a secondary school PE teacher, Lobsang Norbu, on the half volley from the edge of the area.

Tibet lost 4-1, which, under the circumstances, was a massive achievement. The teams had been level at 1-1 at half time, but a more physical and conventional Greenland team eventually took over, driven by their own passions, and playing in front of huge red banners reading 'Free Greenland'. Like Tibet, Greenland later joined CONIFA.

"It was a perfect match between two states that were both famous for their ancient culture, and both had been occupied by colonial powers," Nybrandt remembers. "Spectators flew the flags of both nations. I firmly believe that 60 percent of them had never attended a football game before."

Tibetan football in its modern form started with a bang, then, but then faded with a whimper. The side didn't play a true international game between 2013 - the 100th anniversary of the sport being introduced to Tibet on a British military base - and the build up to the 2018 CONIFA World Football Cup. The prospect of a return was beginning to look unlikely, beyond the side's annual attack on India's Sikkim Gold Cup.

In that competition, an Indian national event which Tibet plays in almost every year, the 2018 team defeated CRPF Jalandhar, an Indian second-tier side from Punjab 7-6 on penalties, before losing narrowly to ultimate winners Mohun Bagan, 1-0 in the closing seconds of the game.

That success, under Tempa Tshering, established the potential of Tibet and played into their CONIFA acceptance for London. The team still train in Dharamshala, the home of the Dalai Lama, though now on a very slightly more impressive pitch on the same location. It's been improved by use and care, and is now lined by adverts for the Lhosa Cup, held around New Year celebrations, which are graffitied across the pitch's walls. The brand of football is limited by the gravel and sand that coats the area's only pitch, but the game is slowly developing a physicality that's long been a competitive issue for the devout Buddhist culture.

The pitch is very literally the only available place to play a full-sized match in the region. Flat land in the hilly north of India is a valuable commodity, and hemmed in by hills on all sides, the team play beneath the symbols of their culture, spectators sat across hilly banks and stupa-like white slopes. The side are a source of plenty of pride: when they formed in 1994, they were the only national representative team in Tibet, in any sport. Playing in Dharamshala is all very pretty, but with huge gaping valleys at one end, it's extremely common to simply lose limited training balls off one end of the stone-walled arena.

President in exile Lobsang Sangay - a man banned from his own country - is particularly proud of the national team. A man with a love of the underdog, he supported Barcelona until they became stronger than Real Madrid, and then switched to Arsenal because of a combination of their recent lack of success and their discipline. His teams, it seems, must be well known enough to make it to Tibet, but not actually win.

"Our team have this dream of going to the World Cup and competing with other countries," Sangay says. "It's not just sport, it's our passion, our cause, our struggle. I think Tibetans are a bit more emotional, and our fans are a bit more fanatical than the usual fan."

"But being a peaceful fanatic, they won't be resorting to any beer drinking and can throwing and such. But there's a lot of passion connected to the team, as they represent our cause."

Passang Dorjee is the Tibetan side's manager. He shies away from the politics of Tibet in conversation, but is a firm advocate for his team. Naturally, all of the team have Tibetan roots, but the 2018 panel are drawn from around the country, with only a handful having crossed the border in their own right.

"We have many players who came from different parts of India, like the south of India Kollegal, Hunsur, Bylakuppe and Mundgod, and from the northern part, places like Clementown, Dharamshala and Delhi," Dorjee says of his side. "Out of the team, a few of them are from Tibet but settled in India like Sangye Gyatso, the assistant goalkeeper is from Tibet, and defender Gelek Wangchuk, I am from Tibet too. We all came from Tibet and studied in the Indian Tibetan Children's Village School, and then went on to higher studies."

"Getting players [traveling] from Tibet is outside of our expectations, and it will be never possible due to all these political problems. It is never possible," Dorjee continues. "We approached FIFA a few years back to get affiliation, but they said we are not able to get that affiliation. Then we registered with CONIFA."

As well as the national team, Dorjee has also been involved in nurturing football in Tibet in general, helping to develop a mentoring process through school and club level games, under the umbrella of the Tibetan National Sports Association. There are now more than 30 clubs involved in the TNSA, with the organisation also developing a women's team.

"The Tibet team fund had been totally based on donations and support from other sources," Dorjee explains. "I have to go to each and every source to get donations. This time, we have strong support from our Central Tibetan Administration too. Any support and sponsorship will be highly appreciated. Presently, I am the only one working on the ground to organize such tournaments and fundraising. We are in exile and we don't have specific sponsors to support us yearly."

On receiving confirmation of their place in London, the manager had called the news "beyond our wildest expectations."

"Our long-term ambitions mean being refugees in exile, we definitely need these kind of platforms for our players. We need to show to the world that there is a Team Tibet, and we can also play. We would like to participate more in international tournaments.

CONIFA members had been really really very very helpful for us in getting this opportunity. They supported us right up until the tournament end, so of course we would like to thank all the executive members of the CONIFA for this unbelievable journey."

Before traveling to London, Tibet were seen off by the Dalai Lama with a blessing in Dharamshala. The spiritual and national leader is himself a symbol of the exiled people's troubles: the kidnapping of his spiritual partner the Panchen Lama as a baby means a century-old cycle of Tibet Buddhist leaders, dating back to the 1390s, will be broken forever when the 83-year-old dies.

The Panchen Lama was a victim of Chinese repression of Tibetan culture, with the second Buddhist figurehead replaced by a Chinese government alternative while he was still a baby. Nobody knows where the preferred Tibetan choice is, or even if he's alive. If he is, it's likely the Panchen Lama is not aware of who he is.

The Dalai Lama, unsurprisingly, has long encouraged his people to maintain their culture and spread its messages across the globe. His message to the team was simple: "Wherever you go, it is very important that you uphold the honour and dignity of Tibet and Tibetan people. Most importantly, carry our values and culture with you as you go."

The Passion of the Hungarians

Szekely Land founded: 2013 *Record Win:* 5-0 v Karpatalya *Record Loss:* 0-3 v Northern Cyprus *Distance Travelled to London:* 1164 miles (1873 kms) *Home Capital:* Targu Mures, Romania *Player Pool Playing In:* Hungary, Romania *CONIFA Ranking:* 5

Karpatalya founded: 2016 *Record Win:* 4-1 v South Ossetia *Record Loss:* 0-5 v Szekely Land *Distance Travelled to London:* 1009 miles (1625 kms) *Home Capital:* Uzhhorod, Ukraine *Player Pool Playing In:* Hungary, Ukraine *CONIFA Ranking:* unranked

There's only one team that can come close to the passion of fans of the Hungarian sides at CONIFA, and that's Northern Cyprus. The difference, of course, is Northern Cyprus - at least in certain circles - are considered to have a genuine and full-on claim on nationhood, and have a huge community of passionate expats behind them. The Hungarian sides are simply representing minority regions, but their fan base have burnt both my shoelaces, and their way into my memory.

The Austro-Hungarian Empire used to be vast, of course, and the result has been a host of CONIFA teams that have drawn a natural affiliation to CONIFA in uncovering their identities. As well as Karpatalya and Szekely Land, there are Felvidek and Delvidek sides also signed up to represent regions of Hungary in Slovakia and Serbia respectively.

The Hungarians reached their footballing peak with Puskas' team of the 50s, a team that could have won a orld cup, and did inflict an unprecedented 6-3 defeat on previously unbeaten-at-home England at Wembley in 1953. Their modern-day footballing impact is substantially smaller, but the passion hasn't waned, and walls and statues dedicated to that 'Match of the Century' and the 'Golden Team' are still easy to track down in Budapest.

Szekely Land's people claim direct descent from Attila's Huns, and likely reside where they do as a kind of border outpost along the Carpathian Mountains, set up centuries ago. They have established a number of impressive rights in Romania, including the right to be educated in Hungarian anywhere where the ethnic population of Hungarians is over 20%. They still hold a passionate connection to their homeland of centuries ago, and march for greater autonomy over Szekely Land every March 10.

Karpatalya has been a hot button issue recently in the Ukraine, too. Early in 2018, the Hungarian Cultural Association in Zakarpattia was twice attacked by arsonists. In response, Budapest spoke of intimidation of Hungarians in the Ukraine, and Kiev suggested that the attacks linked back to a Russian campaign to undermine them, and accused Viktor Orban's government of scaremongering.

The region in question is rural, and its Hungarian populace likely dates back to around the 9th century. It remains an extremely ethnically diverse region.

"A lot of players in our team play in the top division in Hungary, such as Roland Takacs, Istvan Sandor, Gyorgy Sandor, and other players play together for the same club, so for us, the result wasn't a surprise as our strength is playing as a team. The most important thing for us is to play together and fight together as a team," Gergo Gyurki said of his Karpatalya side during the tournament.

"We had just a few training sessions before the tournament, but the manager spoke to us a lot before the tournament started, and that was a very big help for us. That was very important."

"It's a great feeling as we are a Hungarian team, like Szekely Land. It's good meeting other Hungarian players, and it's good to be here and playing for Kárpátalya. It's a very good thing... We try to play from our hearts."

That the two Hungarian sides had to play each other in the semi-finals wasn't an ideal scenario for either of them, as they'd consider themselves to be kin. The scenario divided their support, and forced the pair to compete in a way that didn't really suit. It was emotional, and heady, and at times a little surreal in its atmosphere. The Hungarians were happy to be there, and fielding strong teams that showed the strength behind the two projects. They were insanely passionate about representing their regions.

That passion came out through Karpatalya's goalkeeper Bela Fejer shortly after his side's game against Szekely Land in the tournament semi-finals. Asked about the majority support for Szekely Land amongst Hungarian expats, he said "I cannot contest this. We are from one blood. The way they supported them, in their hearts they supported us as well. We are all Hungarian."

A Word about Russia...

As we've already seen, CONIFA does not go down well in every corner of the globe. Amongst countries with serious objections to the tournament, most have a fairly obvious reason relating to their own sovereignty. These include Sri Lanka (who object to Tamil Eelam), Algeria (who object to Kabylia), China (who object to Tibet), Cyprus (who object to Northern Cyprus), Georgia (who object to Abkhazia), and the Ukraine (whose objections include the sides representing Karpatalya, Donetsk People's Republic, and Luhansk People's Republic).

Outside of the countries involved, most of these objections get little in the way of media scrutiny, mainly. That's probably largely because it comes as a surprise to absolutely nobody that China objects to Tibet's appearance, or Cyprus objects to Northern Cyprus. What does draw attention is the plethora of Russian-linked sides who compete under the CONIFA banner.

Russia, of course, is a political hot potato to many in the western world. There are millions of people who believe Putin's government are working hard to annex various parts of Eastern Europe, backed up by the not insubstantial evidence around the occupation of Crimea in 2014, as well as ongoing suspected (and in some cases proven) activity in other areas bordering Russia. We're not here to discuss Russia's broader geopolitical actions, of course, but CONIFA's.

Sometimes, CONIFA seems to link closely with separatism. Sometimes, they're accused of being a Russian interest entity, pushing separatist, Russian backed states into the limelight. You already know that's not the main reality of CONIFA, but it's an allegation that's hard to ignore. I'll lay out CONIFA's take on the idea, and leave you to judge what's really going on, and what you think of CONIFA's morality.

There are lots of loose connections between CONIFA and Russia, that largely revolve around the Russian connections of the teams in Eastern Europe. There are a number of sides that compete under the CONIFA banner that can be loosely summarised at Russian-backed separatists, including Transnistria (within the borders of Moldova), Abkhazia (Georgia), South Ossetia (Georgia), Donetsk People's Republic (Ukraine) Luhansk People's Republic (Ukraine) and Nagorno-Karabakh (Azerbaijan/ Armenia border).

The existence of these teams is not, in itself, indicative of any Russian backing for CONIFA, of course, any more than the existence of Northern Cyprus is indicative of Turkish backing, or the existence of Tamil Eelam is intrinsically anti-Sri Lankan. Plenty, though, are willing to draw the links they say suggest Russian backing for CONIFA, forcefully enough to require the issue is addressed.

A few weeks after the CONIFA London tournament, an article came out trying to draw those links firmly. Its criticisms ranged from lack of transparency in the way CONIFA is set up (parts of the company are registered in the Isle of Man, which has famously lax financial reporting rules) to a Russian claim that Crimea might host the 2018 tournament (by all in-the-know accounts, this was never seriously considered).

There are other links drawn, too, which vary from tedious to worthy of addressing. On the spurious side, for example, is the fact that Africa Director and Matabeleland boss Justin Walley attended the FIFA World Cup in Russia, and was very positive about his experience, including to Russian media. That's true, but to allege that it shows a link to Russian separatism is utterly daft. Most fans were positive about their experience, and Walley was attending his 6th World Cup, so his attendance at the tournament was almost a given.

On the more sensible end of the allegations are the fact that Dimitri Pagava, a director of CONIFA, is connected with Abkhazia, where the 2016 tournament was hosted, and the possibility that the Russian state had indirectly sponsored the tournament through assistance provided to the Abkhazian government - formally an independent entity, but certainly pro-Russian - during the tournament.

To some, the mere existence of the teams with Russian separatist links is cause for alarm. That's an understandable position: it's not too difficult to argue that no organisation representing a selection of separatist states can really, truly claim to be politically neutral. It's worth noting, though, that CONIFA explicitly bans any kind of separatist statements around its matches, to the extent that the (to most) far more politically palatable slogan 'Free Tibet' is not allowed on the sidelines. If Russia wanted a way to promote these causes, this hardly seems an efficient one.

Let's start with 2016. I don't find Abkhazia's hosting particularly unusual, personally. It makes sense that an organisation hosting a tournament for unrecognised states would try, if at all possible, to have that tournament in one of them. It must also be considered that perhaps as many as half of the entities involved don't have a convincing location that could host such a tournament.

The Russian-connected states make up around 15% of the CONIFA members, and probably 20% of the members that could host a tournament in their region from a facilities point of view, whilst being reasonably accessible to other sides in the tournament and reasonably politically stable.

That one of the four major tournaments so far has been hosted by one of these states is hardly a statistical stretch.

Nevertheless, it's clear that such allegations have to be taken seriously, because they have the potential to undermine the entire basis of CONIFA, and all the good will it's generated. I asked CONIFA General Secretary Sascha Duerkop for his comments on the two key strands of the allegations: that the Isle of Man entity is a money laundering front, and that CONIFA is backing Russian separatism.

We'll start with his comments on the Isle of Man companies, which require quite a complex explanation. They reveal, in fact, the turmoil of CONIFA's financial operations, and give real insight into the difficulties faced in planning such a competition.

"First of all," Duerkop said, "our Sweden-based entity is a non-profit NGO (officially, in Swedish, Idealla Föreningar). Such a non-profit NGO is great to receive membership fees from its members and manage all CONIFA matters in a perfect, transparent and democratic way, which we want. However, non-profits are usually not capable of organizing the operations of an event."

"If you buy 10 litres of beer to sell them in the stadium a month later, the nature of "non-profit" means that you need to write an extensive statement that lays out how this purchase is beneficial for your organizational goals. Additionally, once you sell the beer (usually for a profit), you will need to submit another paper arguing how this is not a profit, which means you need to clearly define that the income of that first pint you sold is being used to cover 1% of the accommodation costs of player X of team Y. All in all, you will have millions of pages of paperwork around arranging a World Football Cup if you do it like this."

"Thus, it became practice, at least in Europe, that sports organizations/clubs usually have a set-up of two legal entities: a non-profit and a business entity. Every Bundesliga club, for example, is set up like this today."

"Then, the non-profit part can receive donations and membership fees and is democratically run with an elected board."

"The business entity, on the other hand, technically receives the rights of a certain event (say, the World Football Cup) for a limited time and is then able to do business with those rights (by selling sponsorships, trading beer and sausages, selling tickets, etc). To get those rights of the non-profit entity, the two entities enter a contract, in which it is defined that all incomes of the for-profit part go as a donation to the non-profit part as a license fee for those rights."

"I know this is complex, but it is business standard, and really just a technicality."

This is how Duerkop outlines CONIFA's starting set up, which is based in Sweden, not the Isle of Man, and not the source of the allegations, though the dual-company set up does seem to be part of the issue identified in the Russian-influenced allegations. I checked with sports accountants, and the set up Duerkop describes is indeed a standard way to organise sporting entities that are part business and part charity.

CONIFA also saw substantial side benefits from the set-up, ones that probably allowed the tournament to continue, albeit at the cost of a bankruptcy, especially at earlier tournaments.

"Now we come to another benefit, although not an intended one, and to the World Football Cup 2014 in Sweden." Duerkop continues.

"In order to operate the Östersund World Football Cup, we founded a limited company in Sweden, which was co-owned by us, the Östersund City Council and Östersunds FK. They were the stakeholders for the event [CONIFA's first]."

"That limited company got all the rights to the World Football Cup 2014 and, by contract, had to cover all its costs. In return, they would share all proceedings."

"The final result of that World Football Cup, was a loss of about €300,000. As a result, the limited company went bankrupt. This was a full business bankruptcy with a court case that went on for three years, but the non-profit did not suffer and remained as it is."

"After the success of Ellan Vannin in the 2014 World Football Cup, and given that we were founded on the Isle of Man and our then vice-president, Malcolm Blackburn, is Manx, the Isle of Man government offered us to settle on the Isle of Man in early 2015."

"They approached Malcolm Blackburn, offering him to give a public grant to CONIFA as 'start up support'. In order to receive that, though, we needed to be an Isle of Man registered entity."

"As our earlier limited company just went bankrupt, we agreed to that and opened two entities on the Isle of Man: CONIFA Ltd, which was intended to be a non-profit, and CONIFA Properties Ltd., the business entity."

"The business entity had a CEO and a physical office for one year, which was mainly covered by the Isle of Man government, and partly by Malcolm Blackburn privately."

"CONIFA Ltd. was intended to become, officially, a non-profit organization, which is crucial to receive donations, for example. However, on the Isle of Man this proved to be impossible. As they do not have company taxes at all, they refuse to give non-profit status to any entity, as it does not make any difference in regards to taxation."

"In addition, we faced major issues regarding banking. The Isle of Man, being a tax haven, has one of the strictest regimes when it comes to banking. We needed nearly a full year to open an account at all and it was only possible when Per-Anders Blind and both vice-presidents (Kristof Wenczel and Malcolm Blackburn) went to the bank in person. They had to prepare a few hundred pages of money laundering paperwork."

This situation was later complicated, of course, by the bitter fall out between the Manx IFA, (who run the Ellan Vannin team), and CONIFA. The disagreement over Barawa's player eligibility described earlier in this book distanced Blackburn from the core of CONIFA: by the time the 2018 tournament came around, Blackburn was no longer a director, but formally he remained an influence as a signatory at the Isle of Man companies.

"Because of the non-profit problem in the Isle of Man, we did initially keep the Swedish non-profit operational," Duerkop explained. "When we tried to move to the Isle of Man completely, half of the membership fees were not accepted by the banks on the Isle of Man."

"No paperwork could convince them to accept funds from Russia (for Abkhazia, South Ossetia, etc), Moldova (for Transnistria) or Iraq (for Kurdistan). Thus, we decided that the non-profit part is useless on the Isle of Man, as it brings too many operational hurdles for us. For every payment we received or sent, we needed a three-page document, hand signed by everyone and posted to the bank."

"We change our plans, closed down CONIFA Ltd and only kept the business part (CONIFA Properties Ltd) on the Isle of Man."

CONIFA Properties Limited is the company that was alleged in some quarters to have been primed to receive Russian money. This allegation revolves around accounts issued for the company which showed an anticipated income of €25,000 that was never received.

CONIFA say this is money they had hoped to receive from sponsorship around tournaments, but never managed to realise. The evidence to suggest anything to the contrary is at best circumstantial, and based around the members of CONIFA, in particular Abkhazia's connection to Russia, and the Isle of Man's relatively closed and inaccessible approach to banking. There is no evidence that any large amount of money ever arrived in CONIFA Properties Limited, let alone from a Russian source.

"CONIFA Properties Ltd. was an empty shell," Duerkop says, laughing off the allegation. "This was because we never received any actual sponsoring money, until late 2017."

"The 2015 European Football Cup in Debrecen was handled by a Hungarian Sports Event company that is owned by Kristof Wenczel (the head of the organization committee) and made a massive loss again. The 2016 World Football Cup was managed by the Abkhazia Football Federation entirely, who could keep all proceeds, but also had to cover all costs (which they did), so no money went over any of our entities."

"The 2017 European Football Cup in Northern Cyprus had the same setup (all managed by the Northern Cypriot FA). Thus, the first time any funds were transferred to or from the account of CONIFA Properties were the sponsoring funds of Paddy Power around Christmas 2017."

"The company did now manage all financials of the most recent World Football Cup (Paddy Power, Eventim proceeds, smaller sponsorings, etc)." Duerkop laid out the account in full, and the details back up his claims. At most, the well-publicised CONIFA/ Russian allegations seem to be something that 'could' have been planned. The reality seems far more pie in the sky. Duerkop admits, though, that the set up was far more complicated than he would have liked.

"That is all more complex than we ever wanted it, and we constantly run into problems with the Isle of Man," he explains. "For the latest World Football Cup, for example, we ended up with a significant amount of cash from on-gate ticket sales. No bank in the

UK accepts that, and the Isle of Man accounts don't have UK clearing banks. Well, they do, but they also accept no cash over £5,000."

"As the Isle of Man is also not part of the EU, you cannot bring the cash in person to the island. In fact, we still have no solution and all the cash, which we desperately need to cover invoices, is just locked up in a safe and we have no clue how to ever use it."

"Such issues and the current issues with Ellan Vannin (Malcolm Blackburn, who manages CONIFA Properties Ltd de facto, is also the president of Manx IFA) resulted in a unanimous decision to finally close down everything on the Isle of Man entirely. Instead, we will set up a new business entity, either in Sweden, Germany or England. We are currently investigating pros and cons."

"At the time, all the moves were straightforward, confirmed by the Annual General Meetings and very logical. In retrospect, they look unnecessary and often plain useless. In fact, we cannot wait to finally leave the Isle of Man, as we felt it was horrible to operate an international organization 'from there', given the huge amount of completely hostile frameworks to do international transactions."

Whether any kind of link with Russia or the Russian government is problematic is a question of interpretation and perspective, of course, but there are certainly a lot of people out there that feel that it is, so I asked CONIFA about those alleged connections, too.

Duerkop openly admits that you can trace a line between CONIFA and Russia at certain times of its existence. His issues with the alleged link - which some view as encouraging Russian separatism - go to the looseness of those links, and the lack of subtlety and perspective in the view that any connection amounts to support of separatism.

"We never had a direct link to the Russian government," Duerkop explains. "However, indirects obviously did exist at times, with mixed results. Let me try to cover them all."

"In 2017, our vice president Kristof Wenczel went to Crimea, as we were invited by the local FA, who hosted a huge conference on the future of football on the peninsula. Now Crimea is Russian occupied".

"At that meeting, representatives of Moscow and the Crimea Republic government were present, and they basically agreed that they would not want to provoke the international football community too much currently, because of the FIFA World Cup that was coming to Russia."

"They urged the Crimea FA to keep a low profile until mid-2018 and then see where they fit in with us (or if they do), as the peninsula is currently in footballing isolation. Teams are not allowed to compete in the Russian or Ukrainian system, currently, and UEFA is basically paying them millions to not do either, and instead run a completely useless local league."

"I also had initial talks with the sports minister of Chechnya about a Chechnyan team. They liked the idea and invited me to meet them in Grozny, but withdrew, as Moscow wasn't keen on the idea and instructed them to not meet me (and wait until the FIFA World Cup is over, again)."

Both of the possible sides mentioned have heavy Russian connections, but CONIFA has dealt with dozens of such potential members, so the connections are hardly surprising, especially given their remit is expressly about representation through football, and doesn't judge approaches based on the politics of the group involved (apart from expressly banning political sentiment around CONIFA itself).

The most prominent links to the Russian state, though, relate to the Abkhazian tournament, which required Russian assistance to go ahead.

"In order to get all teams to the World Football Cup in Abkhazia [back in 2016], the Abkhazian Foreign Minister sent a diplomatic cable to the Russian Foreign Minister, asking him to grant Russian multi-entry visas to all players and other participants to allow them to travel to Abkhazia via Sochi."

"Only thanks to this high-level diplomatic support, we could easily bring in players on all passports, including players on Somaliland passports, which aren't even recognized normally by Russia."

"It is no secret and openly published by the Abkhazian authorities, that a huge percentage of their state budget is coming in from development support financing from Moscow. As the Abkhazian government covered many of the costs of the World Football Cup 2016, and the government had its own costs, such as for security, rebuilding streets for the tournament, and other things, indirectly, it is true that Russia financed part of it."

"However, this was all in the regular budget of the government and only the Abkhazian government decides how they use that budget. It was not an extra budget provided by Russia. In fact, we did ask Russian companies and the Abkhazians invited Russian diplomats, like the Foreign Minister. They all refused to come to not endanger the FIFA World Cup in Russia."

"The only Russians involved in the 2016 World Football Cup in Abkhazia, by the way, were bomb squads that checked the stadiums before every match. The Abkhazian police and army do not have bomb squads and so they asked the Russian army to check the stadiums for bombs, which they did. They always left the stadium two hours before kick-off."

"Last, but not least, I got the same diplomatic visa support as the teams received in Abkhazia to travel to South Ossetia this April."

Duerkop has also shown a strong interest in identity and the Russia Ukraine conflict over the years, and is emphatic in his dismissal of the rumours. "The 'Stop Fake News' portal is a part of a small network of the 'Western Army in the Information War'," he explains of the accusing media outlet. "As much as we are allergic to fake news and propaganda coming out of Russia, we are allergic to the same things coming out against Russia. It's very obviously tendential. We don't think any officials or the public take such publications seriously, so we don't really have any concerns."

It's true, unquestionably, that connections with certain countries on even the most spurious level can be accused of assisting unpopular and at times abusive regimes, with accusations usually coming from the perspective of opposing propaganda. Similar accusations were rife around the FIFA World Cup, typically levelled at supporters who travelled, taking the view that their very presence in Russia assisted Putin. 'Putin's Little Helpers', though, in many cases would probably have attended anywhere in the world, which renders the complaint somewhat moot.

Exploring his own take on the Russia situation, Duerkop says "I personally attended a great round table discussion on 'Frozen Conflicts' in July 2016, after our World Football Cup in Abkhazia, where I discussed things with an advisor of Putin, an advisor of the Ukrainian government and also the vice-head of the EU Foreign Action Service (an equivalent of a "Foreign Ministry")."

"All of them, alongside the OSCE (Organisation for Security and Co-Operation in Europe), the UN and UNESCO very much applauded our work and appreciated what we do, including the high-level Ukrainian diplomat."

"They did propose changes in the wording here and there, but in general came to the conclusion it is a great tool to achieve visibility for the civil society in those places and actually believed it is supporting the 'normal people', even against the 'Russian grip' on some of the regions, as it highlights them and the local independence wishes, not the 'occupation story'."

"If the overwhelming majority of the media, the general public and the highest-level diplomats concerned understand we are not taking a side or standing on a side, I won't worry too much about the exceptions."

"The only effect this might have is that we receive more death threats, something that unfortunately happened from day one of CONIFA regularly, from Sri Lankans, from Turks, from Greeks and so on."

Both for the organisation's personal safety, and from a moral standpoint, even in an open and inclusive organization most would agree there does need to be a line drawn somewhere, though. The question is more where that line resides. I ask Duerkop about connections to countries actually at war, as one example.

"Regarding access to CONIFA, this is a very tricky part," he says. "I openly discussed the topic of Luhansk and Donetsk at the conference on frozen states, as I thought this is the most qualified audience to help in making the right decisions."

"The political/ diplomatic reality is that Donetsk and Luhansk are called 'rebel regions' or similar, while Transnistria, South Ossetia or Abkhazia are called 'de-facto independent states'."

"I tried to understand why that is and the answer was roughly 'that scientists would consider Donetsk and Luhansk a de facto country once it existed for 2 consecutive years in a non-changing boundary. That should be roughly now. In the same time, it is very clear, that the extreme example of the Islamic State (ISIS), for instance, never was a de facto state, as they never had clearly defined borders (but wanted to rule the world)."

"Getting away from those political/ diplomatic definitions, and coming back to CONIFA, we try to look at our members first and put them in the driving seat! Any de facto independent country would, in fact, qualify for CONIFA, as long as it is recognized by a UN member or an existing CONIFA member with de facto independence."

"However, sometimes this is still hard to answer. When Donetsk and Luhansk applied, South Ossetia recognized them, so they would technically qualify, but it was hard to say if it is a long-living de facto state, or just a very fluid troublesome region. Thus, we, as the Executive Committee, did decide to not take any decision and not make any recommendations on the case, but have a discussion with our members and let them decide upon it."

"At that AGM, the Northern Cyprus representative (a country that does not recognize either Donetsk or Luhansk) stood up first and said 'they should both be members. I don't agree with any of the two states, as states, but this is about football. A player in Donetsk or Luhansk currently has no chance to enjoy football in any system and obviously even less to enjoy international football. I know many of you disagree with the independence of Northern Cyprus, but you always agreed to us having a team and we got good friends over the years, as we are a football team and civil society members, not a government. In the same way, I want to give Donetsk and Luhansk a chance and invite them to meet in person and become a member of CONIFA.'"

"Secondly, the (Iraqi) Kurdistan representatives echoed this saying "we have all been rejected and not recognized. Let's do the right thing and not do the same to others now". In the end, the teams unanimously voted for the inclusion of both teams, which surprised us a lot, as we felt it is a tricky one.

"Ultimately, there is no written clear rule that anyone is excluded from CONIFA in general and no one had to drop out because of a current war going on. While I sometimes do personally think about this, it is actually also the way any sport organization always worked. Syrian, North Korean, Turkmen or Eritrean sportsmen do compete in the Olympics, in FIFA and everywhere else. That, in the end, is exactly where sports are and should be. They are 'beyond sport'."

"We would be absolutely open to any team from Russia that doesn't feel Russian joining us [as well as the teams that are from outside Russia, with Russian connections]. In fact, we had such talks with Chechnya, with Ingushetia and a few others before. Also, one of our members, the Lezgian People, are mostly based in Russia (Dagestan mainly) and are a minority rights organization based in Moscow. In short, we are absolutely open to more, yes!"

The argument, from those who disapprove of CONIFA, most often hinges on whether having a football team representing a region enhances their claim to nationality or otherwise. CONIFA, unsurprisingly, claim that fielding a football team is not politically important when it comes to its broader impact, and that it's simply about playing the game and having the option to be represented.

In August 2018, as I penned this book, however, FIFA yet again showed its political angle, by banning Palestinian FA head Jibril Rajoub for his comments on Argentine star Lionel Messi. Rajoub had encouraged Palestinian fans to burn Messi shirts after Argentina agreed to play a friendly with Israel, and was banned from his role for 12 months. Such a comment would not be possible within CONIFA without similar punishment, which does seem to suggest that despite its more perilous position, CONIFA is no more political than the main footballing world body.

That said, if it could be said to encourage separatism, it's understandable that certain quarters would take issue.

"I do not believe that a football team could be directly used to further a separatist agenda, no." Duerkop says. "What our teams often achieve is that they bring all the people of the concerned nation - which is not the same as country - together."

"The Abkhazian national team in 2016, for example, included ethnic Abkhazian, Georgian, Ossetian, Armenian and Russian players. Thus, the whole country, which usually does have debates and splits along those ethnic lines, came together to support the team and they all united behind it.

"That power, to unite people of a defined 'nation', could of course be misused by addressing that then freshly close-knit community and pushing them either way. However, this is exactly where CONIFA kicks in and prevents political messaging. If you read the addresses of the Abkhazian (or Northern Cyprus) President/ Prime Minister in the stadiums of the tournaments in the countries, they always focus on "being all together here", "celebrating football" and "finally being allowed to compete internationally and welcoming the world here".

"Never would we allow a single word "against" anyone else. All our members and teams do not only observe that rule, but demand that rule.

*

So, are the Russian connections cause for concern? I'll let you be the judge of that. The only observations I'd make on the matter are that I don't think it's reasonable to imply that the existence of a football team representing a region is likely to seriously enhance its calls for a separate identity in any meaningful way. If you were looking to forge a route to national independence, football is simply not the route you'd go down: it's so leftfield, disconnected from the natural political order, and - at least at CONIFA's level - lacking in any kind of real political influence. The existence of the sides is at best symbolically important, but does allow people who'd otherwise be kept away from competitive international contests to represent who they feel they are with real pride.

That might not be as politically pure as CONIFA would like, and I can see how that's of little consolation to the Ukraine, who feel they're being undermined. It would certainly help CONIFA if they could persuade a region like the Crimean Tatars to field representation, but it could be difficult in its very nature to persuade a team from a region like that to join an organisation that already features the teams it does. The primary issue, perhaps, is one of 'who joined first'.

My own mind was made up in an interview with Duerkop that took place before I became aware of the Russian-link allegations, in which he outlined his own political neutrality by using a Russian-connected example. Duerkop said his personal view on the authenticity of claims to nationhood was not important, but expressed his personal view on the claims of two different sides.

One was the Chagos Islands, a team representing an Indian Ocean island that was taken over for military purposes in the late 60s and early 70s, its residents evicted by the US and the UK. He said he personally supported their position. His other example? Donetsk People's Republic, a group whose claim Duerkop hinted he didn't agree with. If the organisation were Russian-backed, it's hard to imagine a comment like this - delivered in a candid, 'expanding on a topic' moment - would have been the one he'd chosen.

Justin Walley, who managed the Matabeleland side at CONIFA 2018 and acts as the African director, was one of the core targets of accusations that CONIFA were politically biased, or perhaps 'useful idiots', when the idea gained some traction online. Walley has lived a highly unconventional life residing all over the globe, one that simply doesn't fit with that narrative at all.

"I've been extremely fortunate to travel to over 125 countries and territories in my life." Walley said after his Russian adventures at the FIFA World Cup drew attention on Twitter.

"I've reported on positive experiences from Indonesia to Tajikistan, Sierra Leone to Bolivia. But only my positive words about my visit to Russia World Cup have caused such a crazy reaction. Why?" Why indeed.

Is CONIFA Here to Stay?

Historically, there have been a huge number of non-FIFA tournaments for international, or near-international football teams. Names from the past vary from the fairly well-established, like the VIVA World Cup, to obscure tournaments like the Coupe de l'Outre-Mer (a now defunct tournament for French overseas territories), to the Clericus Cup (the real-life incarnation of Father Ted's famous competition, between Catholic seminaries), and the Inter Island Cup (played between the Cocos Islands and Christmas Island).

The concept dates back as long as FIFA have refused to admit anyone, and in some cases, entirely despite the established organisational home of international football. In fact, CONIFA's predecessor, the NF-Board existed for a decade, twice as long as CONIFA has managed at the time of writing. The Island Games, a competition for small island nations, have existed since 2001.

Throughout its entire existence, though, NF-Board had a total of 27 teams involved, many of whom later transferred over to CONIFA after the collapse of NF-Board and their VIVA World Cup. Those teams included Sealand, who were comically effective in winning five of their twelve games, given they represent a single offshore oil rig in the North Sea with no permanent residents and a land area of 0.004 square kilometres, unrecognised by any other state. Though they do have their own currency.

CONIFA rejects the gimmickry of NF-Board. They rejected an application from Sealand, and have also seen other micronation NF-Board members like the tiny north Italian town of Seborga and Gozo, the second largest island in Malta, fall by the wayside.

CONIFA is already stronger than the NF-Board ever was, in terms of numbers, with almost twice as many members. It's also intrinsically stronger, in that it lacks the novelty factor that NF-Board had around the fringes: they might not all be that good at football, but all CONIFA's members can make sensible claims to - at the very least - a tangible, historic regional identity.

Contests like this don't come together easily, however, and a lot of risks still stand out. While teams were bullish about their appearance ahead of the tournament, that all 16 teams arrived in London (even accounting for the two late replacements) was an astonishing achievement.

The sponsorship was an issue exacerbated by interference from powerful people. The teams continued participation depends on their confidence in the organisation to continue to deliver. It's gone well, so far, but with an extremely limited budget, the potential for political turmoil around every corner and the loose rules that saw Ellan Vannin depart show there's no guarantee things will always run so smoothly.

There's also a growing risk of dilution of concept: without passing any specific judgement on the validity of a host of UK teams, for example - and they seem to be coming - what's to stop such teams exploiting the qualifying system, playing each other regularly, and effectively excluding the more isolated entities? That's a problem, perhaps, that could be dealt with at the time.

At present, CONIFA has no paid employees. It relies on donations, goodwill, and ticket sales. It's quite incredible that the organisation has come through so many challenges already, but it's by no means certain that it will continue to do so.

A Strange Press Conference

It's the day before the CONIFA World Football Cup final, and the cinema/ presentation space in the basement of the north London accommodation the teams are shacked up in has been converted into an impromptu press conference.

There's a strange feel to events like this: like much sport at a less than peak level, journalists can get almost unlimited access to players and officials on the pitch, with the obvious added benefit of getting to take in a game at the same time. And the accommodation is quite out of the way.

As I sit waiting with about a dozen other journalists for things to get underway, it quickly becomes clear that Karpatalya won't actually be sending a representative. In fact, bizarrely, they've sent a player from their defeated semi-final opponents to represent them, in the form of Szekely Land's former Hungarian international Csaba Csizmadia.

Discussions, generally, are along broad themes, but do highlight some interesting aspects of the tournament, and give an insight into where people think the stories are.

"We've got used to being around the top," manager Bülent Aytaç says of Northern Cyprus' hopes. "It's a pleasure to be there, because this is the only chance we get to play abroad. It's an honour to represent our country."

The route to Karpatalya's inclusion was given in detail: the system is a sort of continental quota, which saw the Hungarian ethnicity side replace Felvidek at late notice. "They automatically got into the tournament. They were more or less ready, but it was very hard work for the management," Kristof Wenczel of CONIFA's executive explained. "It was very hard work for the management as they had other plans; they are involved in bringing Real Madrid's junior team to Hungary, so couldn't be in London. The team itself was completed right before the tournament."

"The general process is we first have a continental split according to the number of members, and then there was a replacement list. If a team drops out, we call the first team, the second team, the third team and so on," Duerkop continued. "In this case the first team took the place. We're always conscious of these issues and we have to be prepared, and have it clear who is the first team, the second team. It becomes part of the communication."

"It's very funny, it seems to be good to be a replacement team. In 2014, the County of Nice came in at four weeks' notice and they won the tournament. We are kind of surprised, we saw Karpatalya in Northern Cyprus [in the European Championships] last year and they looked good, but they've really stepped up a level this time."

Northern Cyprus were keen to play up the support they've received during the tournament. The team are used to playing in a relatively isolated football league. A majority of their players play for Northern Cypriot clubs who play in the KTFF Süper Lig, one of very few 'national' (pretending on your politics) leagues in Europe that don't act as feeders into European competition, meaning the players don't get to play abroad in the normal course of their playing careers. Other such leagues include the Abkhazian league and Crimea's football league.

The league has been established for more than 60 years, and holders Yenicami Ağdelen (North Nicosia), Mağusa Türk Gücü S.K. (Famagusta) and Doğan Türk Birliği (Limassol) provide a majority of the squad. All the players are based in Northern Cyprus, with the exception of burgeoning Galatasaray youngster Ahmet Sivri (who left Yenicami for the Galatasary youth system in 2017) and London based Necati Gench.

"This is not political for us," says boss Bülent Aytaç, "but it's great to connect with the community in London. For some, they might follow Turkey, but Turkey will never really be their team. This is about showing ourselves and playing football. How can you tell a 15-year-old boy he can't ever play top-level football, because of politics?"

"CONIFA has made everything easy for us. In the stadiums they are supporting us. They're not used to playing abroad very much. It's very important that when we leave the country, and we play in front of spectators from another country that we make the right impact. I think it's a very big, strong team we have. All the players are from Northern Cyprus' league apart from two, so we are showing our football ability. This is the only way we can go out and play matches abroad."

"In North Cyprus they really love football. We have a lot of young people playing and enjoying the game. They can see the world through the internet, and reach everything easily. You can't tell them they can' get involved. We don't care about the politics, we just want to play football."

It's hard to imagine a similar conversation ahead of a standard international match. Even notoriously weak international sides like San Marino and Gibraltar are rarely asked to justify their existence in international terms - at most, they're asked if it might be better for them to play in a lower-tier grouping set up. Northern Cyprus has a population of over 300,000, around ten times that of UEFA members Gibraltar (who they'd likely beat, too), and constantly find themselves justifying their very existence in the footballing world.

Matchday 6: completing the full set

When I planned the writing of this book, one of the things that played into the madness of the match planning was a little personal ambition: to try and catch every team. On match day five I'd realised this was achievable, with a few provisos: I needed to head for Sutton really early ahead of the semi-finals to catch Panjab (a game I had to leave after 60 minutes), and I needed Tibet and United Koreans In Japan to play each other on the final day.

The latter scenario looked likely: United Koreans In Japan were almost certain to be overmatched against 2016 Champions Abkhazia in their placement game, though Tibet and Kabylia could probably go either way.

As it turned out, Kabylia got it together and thumped Tibet, and Abkhazia saw off United Koreans In Japan as expected, so I found myself in an oddly quiet, suburban area just south of the Thames - central London, but with a different feel - watching the two sides I hadn't yet seen in person face off.

It was the day of the final, and a comfortable familiarity had settled over the tournament for the regulars. A few hundred had turned out for the game, and amongst them were the towering, enthusiastic figure of Panjab FA boss Harpreet Singh, the enthusiastic commentators following their team from Kings Langley, Cascadia's impassioned advocates, and the regular Tibetan followers from Bristol Rovers.

I talk to the Bristol Rovers fans, and no one's quite sure how the link between their side and Tibet came about, though they are concerned it's had some unintended consequences. "There were rumours of a Chinese takeover at one point," a fan in the white and blue quarters of the western club told me. "It might have brought a lot of money to the club, which would be nice because we've always struggled with that side of things. I heard someone pointed out the Tibet connection, and that was the end of it."

There might be a little tinge of regret in what he says, but the connection is still passionately advocated for. There are three or four flags around the ground bearing both the Bristol Rovers badge and the colourful red and blue colours of Tibet. A bunch of kids are having a game in the only open space around the side of the pitch, where a five-a-side goal is the hub for an impromptu contest between kids in Bristol Rovers shirts and kids in the Tibetan national colours.

There are few supports quite like the Tibetan one. The national shirt is a genuine collector's item, going on ebay for a small fortune, yet there are at least fifty of the blue and red sun strips, Tibet written jaggedly on the back of the collar, spread around the St Paul's ground.

The Koreans are conspicuous by their absence, seemingly represented by the team themselves, coaches, and a single buzzing reporter. The Koreans are clearly the better team, but are blighted by the same problem that has seen them playing for eleventh or twelfth come the end of the tournament (Tibet's elevation to this status is largely connected with their walkover against Ellan Vannin).

There are around 600,000 people of Korean origin living in Japan, their background a mix of North and South Korean, or, in many cases, not really either, their ancestors having emigrated before the peninsula split in the early 50s. In fact, many Zainichi moved specifically because of the splitting of Korea, and they tend to be very pro a unified Korea, a demand that is fading fast in Korea itself. While polls have shown all but the most elderly in modern day South Korea are no longer in favour of a unified north and south of the country due to the weight of the potential economic influences (typically the primary reason), the United Koreans wear the outline of the entire Korean peninsula, undivided, on their shirts.

The younger members in particular are known locally as Zainichi, the Japanese label for a group of Korean foreigners getting by in Japan on a series of temporary residency visas, with no intention to go home. Their training facilities as a team are world class, but a little digging into their social scenarios quickly reveals why the identity has stuck so firmly.

187

Korea and Japan have a complex and hostile past, including a period in which Korean women were used by Japanese soldiers as sex slaves, during a period of Japanese occupation and rule over Korea. The Koreans are looked down on by the Japanese, at least according to many Koreans.

The dislike of Koreans in Japan is often linked to the ability of North Korea to strike Japan - supposedly - at short notice, something that causes fear, especially on the west coast of Japan. Some Koreans hide their heritage, which could involve changing their distinctive three-syllable Korean names - in order not to suffer from what they believe to be deeply ingrained persecution, passed down through generations. The language is often dropped even within families in Japan for the same reason.

Their environment, though, is perfect for a representative football team, with top class facilities and even a club team, FC Korea, who have played in the Japanese league since the 60s, to pick their team from. They currently play in the Kanto league, covering Tokyo and the surrounding areas, the Japanese fifth tier.

Ahn Yong Hak, a former North Korean World Cup international and manager of the United Koreans, explains "My ancestors lived here after the Korean War. There are many difficulties and it is challenging living in Japan. I don't have Japanese residency."

"Football has been the bridge between our countries, Japan, North and South Korea. North Korea and Japan don't have great relations. Every time news about North Korea is broadcast, the atmosphere gets worse. I don't have the rights that Japanese people have. I am Zainichi Korean and a North Korean passport holder, so it is very difficult for me."

"Every time I visit a country, I have to get a visa. Even with a visa, I am always stopped by customs because they have never seen a North Korean passport before. Even though I was a professional player, I could not visit the USA."

"Since I started playing football from six years old, it's been my dream to play in the FIFA World Cup. It was very exciting walking onto the pitch in South Africa. The Portugal game was a miserable game [North Korea lost 7-0]. I played as hard as I could, so I don't regret anything."

"The articles in the western media that the players were sent to the mines after South Africa are not true. The goalkeeper that played with me is still the national team's goalkeeper. He wouldn't be if he was sent to the mines!"

Kim Jong Un is a young leader and very interested in football, and supports the country. The Western media is very negative about him. I hope that some more positive news will reach the world," he concludes.

In St Paul's the proficient Koreans knocked the ball around comfortably, but frantic Tibetan defence largely got the better of them as they tried to play in a cutting final ball, with most of their efforts pelted in from distance as the Tibetans stood firm.

The Tibetans took their first lead of the tournament against the run of play, with Tenzing Yougyal sliding the ball under the Korean 'keeper after a winding run by Kelsang Dhuntsok. The lead seemed to give the Tibetans confidence: suddenly they were a fluid, attacking side putting the flailing Koreans under substantial pressure, egged on by a fanatical backing.

The United Koreans came back into the game in a big way in the second half, and while Tibet held on for extended periods of pressure, the Koreans equalised when a corner from Byun Yeong Jang was turned into the Tibetan goal through a mishit clearance with just six minutes remaining.

Further pressure didn't tell for the Koreans, so the game went to penalties, with the first Tibetan penalty taker smashing the ball home and ripping off his shirt to tense his muscles in front of the Tibetan end. It wasn't to be for the fashionable underdogs, though, as the Koreans hit four from four to take the shootout 4-1, after a couple of tame finishes from the Tibetans. Tibet hadn't got their win, but had charmed almost everyone they'd come into contact with.

Matchday 6: It all comes down to this...

The queue to get into Enfield's Queen Elizabeth II Stadium trails back about 100 metres, stretching across Donkey Lane and into the park in a blaze of unrecognisable football shirts and colourful multiculturalism.

CONIFA has caught the imagination: the Turkish Cypriot community is out in force, plastered in red and white, stars and crescent moons. Their opposite number, Karapatalya, have not been well supported in London, but have found a vocal backing for the final. Ten minutes before kick-off, one end of the awkward stadium, just a few feet behind the goal, is alive with green, red and blue flares and boisterous chanting.

Most of the teams are here, too. Abkhazian players and fans occupy one end of the main stand, a huge flag draped over its barriers, while half the Tuvalu squad take turns climbing a tree behind the numerous team buses, hoping for a view of the pitch. Tibetan flags dot the audience, intermingled with Kabylian flags, Padania banners and even a North Korean standard. Cascadia's besuited mega-fan waves a green, white and blue fern-tree at centre-pitch.

On the pitch, the Northern Cyprus kitman is the pre-kick off star. He's died his thinning hair red and spiked it into a multitude of points reminiscent of The Prodigy frontman Keith Flint, and is making his way at speed from one stand to another, pumping up the crowd. Even the rowdy Hungarians behind one goal greet him with rowdy good humour.

There are plenty here who are mainstays at lower-tier football, drop ins for the passion of the event and the novelty of the experience. John 'Village' Atkins, a passionate Barnet supporter and traveller, has continued a habit of draping the pitch side in multinational flags of obscure nations. One corner of the pitch has become a home to the symbols of unrecognised Asian states and smaller nations, with Cambodia, Sri Lanka, Bangladesh and Liberian symbols woven into a powerful display of simple inclusivity.

First the stands are full, and then the barriers. Finally, the grassy banks overlooking Enfield's pitch are crawling with fans trying to catch a view of the first senior World Cup football final held in Britain since 1966. Quite a few matches in the course of the 2018 tournament have had attendances of less than 200, but CONIFA have the atmospheric finale they deserve.

When the teams emerged, they did so from a cage, warming up with a house fire's worth of flare smoke rising behind one stand, where the goalkeeper was in danger of disappearing into the crowded scenery.

Finally, the kitman returned to the Northern Cyprus bench for a well-earned sit down, forward Billy Mehmet appealed for noise from the Cypriot element, Karpatalya emerged from their huddle, and the final was underway.

Very few tournaments conclude with classic contests, and CONIFA's was the same: a nervous, bitty encounter where defences were largely on top, and players seemed most intent on not making a mistake.

The game was played at a frantic pace, but lacked final ball quality. Karpatalya headed over twice from close range, but they were no more than half chances. Tansel Ekingen had a couple of solid chances at the other end, and playmaker István Sándor looped a shot just wide of the fast post from 25 yards. That was it for the first half, though, in a tight contest in which defences took charge.

Northern Cyprus grew into the second half, with Karpatalya 'keeper Béla Fejér scraping the ball from the head of Uğur Gök early on, and Fejér forced to tip over from a header shortly afterwards.

At the other end, György Toma's weaving runs were a constant threat to the Cypriots, as he wove in and out of their defence, several times being denied by last-ditch challenges. Toma is a charging, inventive midfielder who forged his career with Ukrainian top tier side FC Hoverla Uzhhorod, making his debut against Dynamo Kiev. Hoverla Uzhhorod were expelled from the top tier of Ukrainian

191

football due to debts, with Toma denied the chance to make a further impact when his side went out of business.

The forward stood out a mile for Karpatalya, but at the other end the physical presence of boxer-like Billy Mehmet was starting to tell, as Northern Cyprus threatened a breakthrough in the air, aided by Kenan Oshan's deadly long throw.

With ten minutes left on the clock, a break down the right from Northern Cyprus saw Mehmet played in eight yards out, and his diving header - played off the ground - beat Fejér and crashed off the top of the crossbar.

Halil Turan had a great chance with three minutes left with Northern Cyprus firmly in charge of a now frantic finale, but nodded a powerful header high over, and with it ensured penalties.

If the game had been a disappointment, the shootout was nothing of the sort. Gyürki scored for Karpatalya, before Fejér saved a low finish to his left from Mehmet. Karpatalya were two up when Toma hit home, and Kurt saw Fejér guess right and stop again.

Baksa hit the post for Karpatalya and Istvan Sandor saw his shot saved, while Oshan and Ersalan hit two incredibly emphatic penalties to level things up and effectively take things to early sudden death.

Karpatalya had the disadvantage of shooting into an incredibly partisan stand of Turkish Cypriots, but Alex Svedjuk kept his nerve, scoring to his left, before Fejér made an incredible stop from Halil Turan to take the title, taking off in disbelief towards his own men on the half way line.

Like Denmark at Euro '92, Karpatlya hadn't qualified for CONIFA 2018, but they had got the better of most of the top sides in the tournament on the way to winning it.

There was a split second of stunned stillness from Fejér, who's later named player of the tournament, right after his save. Then he was off, charging towards the red and green wave that's powering towards him from the centre circle, arms raised.

They lapped Enfield, ending in front of their own fans at one end as the flares were relit and Northern Cyprus collapsed into the turf. There was a pitch invasion, and the Karpatalyan players bounced in a ring in the middle of their fans.

Some of the players later tell the media that they'd been in the middle of planning summer holidays when the call came for Karpatalya to travel to London, and there were plenty of players who could have represented the Hungarian/ Ukrainians who didn't make the trip.

Alex Svedjuk, who scored the third penalty, said he had a simple hope from the win. "I hope this puts Karpatalya on the map," he said.

Gergo Gyurki added "I think early successes built up the team for the final. It was great teamwork. It's a very great thing for Karpatalja because we are really small. But we played from our hearts to win the tournament for our people."

There was a sombre feeling but a couple of rye smiles as Northern Cyprus collect their gold trophy for second place atop Enfield's main stand, Mehmet biting his lip and the red-haired kit man quiet as they raise the trophy above the remaining fans in the fading light. They're the fifteenth team to emerge onto the balcony: every team in the tournament emerges to receive their acclaim and participation medals.

Karpatalya's response was far more emphatic, as they were presented with their medals by CONIFA staff in the Tibetan Khata, a thin, pale white silk scarf designed to symbolize pure and peaceful intentions in the givers, handed to them by the Tibetan squad.

Fejér led his team to the front barrier, where they jumped up and down, chanting songs about their win. When the trophy rose above their heads, there followed three minutes of unstoppable celebration, and a few tears from the men in red.

But the jubilation isn't just amongst the team. Duerkop was grinning from ear to ear as he passed out medals. Blind hopped from foot to foot as he embraced his team of volunteers. The infectious smiles are everywhere. CONIFA was huge for the winners, but for many others, the glory of it all was that it happened at all.

Which leads us to CONIFA's soul, and the heart of football for many of us who prefer to look beyond the multinational conglomerates. It's not about teams building market share in China, inventing pre-season tournaments to 'be competitive' in new markets, or building squads of sixty to exploit the loan market, like a creepy human-talent based version of a landlord.

At least for me. For me, it's about the men who play for their country for no other reason than the pride and emotion it stirs in them, the symbolism, and the experience.

Matchday 6 Results, Saturday June 9:

Final: Karpatalya 0-0 Northern Cyprus (Karpatalya win 3-2 on penalties)

Third place play-off: Padania 0-0 Szekely Land (Padania win 5-4 on penalties)

Fifth place play-off: Panjab 3-3 Cascadia (Panjab win 4-3 on penalties)

Seventh place play-off: Western Armenia 7-0 Barawa

Ninth place play-off: Kabylia 0-2 Abkhazia

Eleventh place play-off: Tibet 1-1 United Koreans In Japan (United Koreans In Japan win 4-1 on penalties)

Thirteenth place play-off: Matabeleland 1-0 Tamil Eelam

Fifteen place play-off: Tuvalu 3-0 (walkover) v Ellan Vannin

CONIFA World Football Cup 2018: The Final Standings...

(1) Karpatalya (won 4, drawn 2, goals for 15, goals against 5, goal difference +10)

(2) Northern Cyprus (won 3, drawn 3, goals for 17, goals against 6, goal difference +11)

(3) Padania (won 4, drawn 1, lost 1, goals for 21, goals against 5, goal difference +16)

(4) Szekely Land (won 3, drawn 1, lost 2, goals for 16, goals against 7, goal difference +16)

(5) Panjab (won 2, drawn 2, lost 2, goals for 17, goals against 7, goal difference +10)

(6) Cascadia (won 3, drawn 1, lost 2, goals for 17, goals against 11, goal difference +6)

(7) Western Armenia (won 3, drawn 1, lost 2, goals for 12, goals against 8, goal difference +4)

(8) Barawa (won 2, lost 4, goals for 7, goals against 22, goal difference -15)

(9) Abkhazia (won 4, drawn 1, lost 1, goals for 15, goals against 4, goal difference +11)

(10) Kabylia (won 1, drawn 1, lost 4, goals for 8, goals against 15, goal difference -7)

(11) United Koreans In Japan (won 1, drawn 4, lost 1, goals for 7, goals against 4, goal difference +3)

(12) Tibet* (drawn 1, lost 4, goals for 4, goals against 20, goal difference -16)

(13) Matabeleland* (won 2, drawn 1, lost 2, goals for 5, goals against 12, goal difference -7)

(14) Tamil Eelam (won 1, lost 5, goals for 4, goals against 22, goal difference -18)

(15) Tuvalu* (lost 5, goals for 4, goals against 24, goal difference -20)

(16) Ellan Vannin* (withdrew) (won 2, lost 1, goals for 6, goals against 3, goal difference +3)

* Records do not include goals or results from 3-0 'awarded games' in which Ellan Vannin did not participate, or the replacement friendly games organised for teams who should have played Ellan Vannin.

CONIFA 2018: the fall out

Ellan Vannin are no longer excluded from CONIFA competition as of January 2019, after a CONIFA members' vote. Both CONIFA and the Isle of Man side continue to blame each other over Barawa's squad issues, and Ellan Vannin's subsequent withdrawal.

Northern Cyprus, Ellan Vannin and Tuvalu all consider joining FIFA a long-term goal, though Northern Cyprus and Ellan Vannin in particular acknowledge such recognition looks some way off. Jersey, an island off the south of the UK, was rejected in an application for recognition by UEFA in early 2018, on the basis that the island is not an independent state. Their status as a British Crown Dependency is extremely similar to the Isle of Man's. They've now joined CONIFA, alongside Cornwall.

Harpreet Singh and his Panjab side continue to focus on the promotion of south Asian players in British football, an area in which there remains a concerning lack of success at a professional level.

Karpatalya returned home victorious, but not everyone was happy. Sports Minister for the Ukraine, Igor Zhdanov, released a statement on his Facebook page following Karpatalya's victory, calling for the most draconian of treatment of the players involved on their return.

"I call on the Security Service of Ukraine to respond appropriately to such a frank act of sporting separatism. It is necessary to interrogate the players of the team, as well as to analyse in detail the activities of the deputy organizer of the 'Carpathian' for the purpose of encroachment on the territorial integrity of Ukraine and ties with terrorist and separatist groups," he said.

The Ukrainian Football Association (FFU) also signalled their intent to act against the squad, releasing an official statement on their website:

"According to the results of a review, sanctions will be applied against these players, in particular disqualification, after which players will not be able to claim to participate in amateur or professional tournaments held on the territory of Ukraine under the auspices of the FFU."

"We also urge the law enforcement agencies of Ukraine to pay attention to the fact of participation of the indicated players in competitions organized by CONIFA and to check their actions on the subject of propaganda of separatism and encroachment on the territorial integrity and inviolability of Ukraine."

Responding to the statement, CONIFA explained, "CONIFA wishes to stress that it is a politically-neutral, volunteer-run charity registered in Sweden. CONIFA takes no position on the political status of its member associations. CONIFA wishes to state that, to the best of its knowledge, the players, administrators and officials of the Karpatalya football team have never expressed any separatist sentiments or ambitions. The team has a long-standing, demonstrable history of publicly embracing the region's dual heritage; the team's flag and logo contain both flags, while the team wears Ukrainian and Hungarian colours on the pitch."

Fortunately, of the 22-man winning squad, 20 play their football for Hungarian teams, and 1 in Romania. The final player, 46-year-old goalkeeper Szergej Petranics, retired immediately after the tournament. The FFU's decision has no immediate impact. Thirteen of the 25, however, are 25 or under, and many of them born in the Ukraine, so it's likely to limit their future options.

Bizarrely, this attack by Ukrainian representatives came alongside a social media rumour that many of the Carpathian players were not in fact of the Hungarian/ Ukrainian origin they claimed at all. Three minutes of research proved this rumour to be entirely false.

Sides from Yorkshire to the Chagos Islands have declared their intent to turn up at CONIFA 2020, and are already planning how to navigate the tournament's somewhat convoluted qualifying process. The CONIFA executive hope they will be joined by the organisation's first ever representative from South America, and are in touch with teams in Brazil and Panama that have expressed an interest.

As for Matabeleland, they continued their crowdfunding exercise, including at the gates of the final game in Enfield. They used the huge public goodwill they generated at the tournament to scrape together the cash to do a quick tour of London before they returned to their lives in Zimbabwe. They chose to see Buckingham Palace, Trafalgar Square, and, naturally, Arsenal Football Club.

Epilogue

It's a cold September as I write this, and another season of the Premier League is kicking in, the charge being led by the usual selection of expensively-assembled, corporate-backed clubs where salaries read like lottery wins, and whether a team in red beats a team in blue, for some reason, resonates on an almost global scale.

I don't begrudge those who find passion in this. I used to, too, and still know enough about the upper echelons of the game to hold down a pub conversation, or check out how the goals flew in. But talent shouldn't be everything, and money certainly shouldn't be everything, and I think we can all acknowledge the ever-growing power of the sporting dollar, the unstoppable march towards things like the European super league, and third-tier clubs as little more than top-tier feeder clubs fuelled by a 'take a punt on youth - all the youth' loan system.

I'm one of those people who believes football should be about more. It should have the power to change, rather than become an unaffordable luxury, played out on Sky TV and watched from shiny corporate boxes where chatter and sandwiches are as important as what happens on the pitch. Most of all, it should have passion: not just in the key games, the finals, and the high-level national sides, but be oozing with meaning for those lucky enough to pull on the shirts they longed for as kids. And for me, it just isn't. Not anymore.

There are many like me. Call us fallen football fans, or purists, or ideologues, or whatever your preferred insult for the overly cynical might be, but a sport that can be played almost anywhere, with almost no equipment, should be for all. It's an interesting side note of the game that so many of its stars come from relative poverty.

There's a growing love for the underdogs: FC St Pauli, FC United of Manchester, AFC Wimbledon, Dulwich Hamlets and San Marino. Team that don't really need, or expect, to win. They simply mean more to those who follow them, and the stark reality is that if they were to win, and see the influx of fans that comes with the status, it may well all be ruined anyway.

It's from that kind of thought process that this book emerges. I love football. Always have. But the teams I watch most often are Crumlin United and Liffey Wanderers, St Patrick's Athletic and Tolka Rovers. My fiver, or tenner, matters to them, and so does their team, often built from the ground up on a group of mates playing together since they were kids, and competing to win leagues that most football fans will happily dismiss flippantly as they finish off their pints.

But so many stars, now lost in millionaires' rows, far from those youthful jumpers for goalposts and friendships embedded in kicking around a piece of leather, never got that chance to dream. Even for those who did get to dream, those dreams are too often dead alongside the first hint of adulthood. Don't make a pro team by the age of 16, and your shot at the footballing big time is already a shot at that proverbially lottery.

That's where CONIFA starts to matter, and why it needs to grow. I'm contemplating another set of predictable top-tier results on another Sunday afternoon when the latest breakthrough flashes across my social media.

Darfur have a new side.

The refugee side, forged in the heart of a squalid camp in the deserts of Chad, central Africa, appeared at the first CONIFA World Football Cup in 2014, where they proved to be the tournament whipping boys, conceding no less than 61 goals across four games.

It's hard to think of a case where winning or losing so transparently didn't matter as that of the Darfur side. They got to play an international tournament in Sweden, after many in their ranks had seen members of their family die, struggle for food, struggle for homes and be forced to flee their country. Pulling on that shirt for the first game can only have been something quite special.

Darfur United still exist, run by aid organisations in the same refugee camps that saw the team start out half a decade ago, and no doubt catering to many of the same people. Their latest expansion is a simple one, and one repeating itself around the CONIFA world (Sapmi and Matabeleland have also followed suit): a women's team. The Darfur team comes about through the purest of stories. With the men's team, known as Darfur United, practising regularly in the camps, crowds were gathering to watch them play. Passion for the game is clear in the camps, where games take place without the most rudimentary of equipment, including shoes.

Pictures from the early days of the Darfur United recruitment drive back in 2012 show scrappy football tops and plain t-shirts with the names of the games' stars written in marker on the back. The yet-to-be-fully-formed team kick a ball around on dirt pitches, where every play is accompanied by a puff of dusty sand flying into the air. The camp in its entirety survives largely on donated clothes, food, and other charitable offerings.

With the men's side taking off, though, the women started copying their skills on the sideline, and asking why they weren't being included. Now, shortly after forming, they'll be looking for their own competitive outlets. Meanwhile, the men are heading for the Human Rights Cup in Johannesburg, South Africa, and, for most of the current players, getting a first taste of competitive football. They'll be joined by teams like Golden Girls Football Centre (from Mogadishu, Somalia) and FFA Global Maramba (from Livingstone, Zambia).

Naturally, I reach out to find out what's going on. Gabriel Stauring, Founding Executive Director of a charity called iACT, is behind the story.

"I started to hear about Darfur, and what was beginning to be called "genocide", in 2004," he tells me. "It was the 10th anniversary of the Rwandan genocide, and it just hit me that I had done nothing during that horrible event in human history. I decided that I had to find a way to participate to make things better this time around."

"I never intended to work full time on this and be the founder of a humanitarian organization. As I became involved and then decided to visit the camps in 2005, there was just no turning back. We first became advocates for the people of Darfur—sharing their stories

203

with anyone willing to listen (and even with those not so willing). We began supporting refugees on areas that they saw as the most important to their lives: education and activities that empowered them, gave dignity, and offered hope and joy for them and their children."

"From there it evolved to co-creating actual programs with the refugees, programs such as Little Ripples (a preschool program that is led and run by refugees). That first trip in 2005 was going to be my only trip to the region. I thought I'd be able to then move on and 'continue' with my life. I'm about to go on my 30th trip to those camps."

The Darfur football team came later, and - as has almost always been the case with the game - the women's team later still.

"The women, refugees living in the camps, requested - actually demanded - a team of their own," Stauring says. "When they saw the men trying out for the first Darfur United Team, from the sidelines the women called me over and said 'What about us?! We want that!'"

"We first worked with them in creating the Refugees United Soccer Academy (RUSA), and women took on the coaching responsibilities. In the eight camps where the Academy now exists, they were excited to have the opportunity and showed great courage and eagerness to take on a sport they had never practiced before. There might have been some nerves, but all they showed was determination."

"Soon, we are heading out to the same refugee camp where the Darfur United Men's Team held its first try-outs. All RUSA women coaches will join us there, along with a few others that express an interest, and we will hold the first try-outs and training for the DU Women's Team. We will then leave them with a training program so that they can prepare for competition in the future."

"We do hope to have the Darfur United Women's Team compete within the soon to be formed CONIFA women's structure. That will take some time, though. For our group, they are starting from the very basics of learning the sport. Ideally, we want them to train for some months and then find them some games to participate in within Chad, maybe in the capital where there is some structure for women football players."

"We'd also love to bring teams from the outside - maybe CONIFA Teams - to play in one of the refugee camps. It would mean so much to the population to see their team play. I can only imagine what it would mean to a girl to see an all-women's team competition!"

"Eventually, we do want them to travel and compete in a CONIFA World Cup, just like the men."

"Funding is a very big issue. We currently rely on donations to fund all activities. We are working hard to find bigger support and sponsorships."

I ask Stauring about the camps in Chad, and immediately becomes apparent why funding is such a problem.

"Eastern Chad - right on the border with Darfur - is one of the most remote and harshest places on earth," he says. "It's on-the-edge living for anyone out there, but then you must add the stress of being refugees that are confined to camps with little freedom of movement or opportunity. Food rations have been cut drastically in these camps, as have other services, and refugees are struggling on a daily basis to provide for the basic needs of their families."

"The pitches are a space with sand and rocks. We emphasize at RUSA that the coaches must make it safe for the children, as they play barefoot, but it's nothing like the fields here in the USA, with beautiful grass or turf. Outside of RUSA, the resources are basically zero. Children play with homemade footballs, which they kick with their bare feet. "

"For the women, it's the first time that they are given an opportunity to break away from their very defined gender roles. Women do most of all the work in the camp, from building the homes, to collecting firewood and water, to cooking and washing, and taking care of the children and elderly. But aside from this, when they took the opportunity, they just love to play. They experience the joy of playing, competing, and teamwork."

"Traditionally, girls and women do not play soccer in Darfur. There were some leaders (and some community members) that did not feel comfortable in seeing females participating in what they saw as a sport for males. We had conversations about how the sport is good for the girls and women, but also for the entire community."

"More importantly, refugee leaders that know the power of equality took on the responsibility of sharing that information with their own community, and that started to change perceptions and attitudes. There are now thousands of girls playing soccer in the camps, led by sixteen amazing refugee women coaches. These same women will be a part of the first team. They are trailblazers in the sport and in creating positive change for their community."

"Nutrition in the camps, or the lack of proper nutrition, is a big issue. Rations have been cut drastically over the years, and there are very few opportunities for the refugees to make up the difference. We provide salaries to our RUSA coaches, so that gives them a steady source of income for them and their families."

"With the men's team, we definitely saw the effects of long-term nutritional imbalance. We do the best that we can to support them and offer information (in addition to the salaries for the coaches that will become the players), but we are still learning and know that this is something we need to continue to address."

"The big plans are to continue supporting the refugees (from Darfur and other areas affected by violence) and their aspirations. Football is a beautiful tool for change. I can't wait for the day I see the Darfur United Women's Team, wearing their full kits, step on to a pitch representing their people. We will work next to the refugees and have them take on bigger positions of responsibility—on the management and coaching side of things."

When the ladies' team time comes, many of the players will be competing in shoes for the first time, on grass for the first time, and they'll probably be losing, most likely heavily. But as we know already, that's just not the point.

What's next?

CONIFA continues in 2019 with another European tournament, which will take place in the region of Artsakh, a de facto independent territory on the border of Armenia and Azerbaijan that won its independence as a result of the end of the Nagorno-Karabakh war in 1994. The region is chasing FIFA membership, but remains unrecognised by the international community.

The Nagorno-Karabakh War is thought to have killed upwards of 30,000 people, and as well as Azerbaijan and Armenia, also drew in Chechen Militants, the Turkish army, armament supply from Russia, Ukraine, Israel and Greece. There is no formal peace treaty, and Turkey has enforced a blockage on Armenia since a year before the end of the war.

CONIFA are excited about the tournament. "After the incredible success of London 2018, we are excited to be taking our next tournament to a beautiful and relatively undiscovered part of the world," CONIFA President Per-Anders Blind said of the decision. "During several official delegation visits to Stepanakert, CONIFA has received incredible hospitality. We are confident that participating teams, fans and travelling media will enjoy the same experience next year."

Twelve teams will contest the tournament, with the bulk of matches expected to take place in Stepanakert, the petite capital, a city with a population of 55,000 and known mainly for its Armenian cultural art. From an international political perspective, the region is part of Azerbaijan.

CONIFA will also host its Annual General Meeting in 2019 in Kawkow, Poland, and is likely to see CONIFA further expand as a result of new applications. The 2020 World Football Cup will also be in the planning stages, and staring over the horizon.

The continued existence of CONIFA isn't easy. As you read this, they may be yet to transfer the cash takings from their London tournament out of its holding location in a London safe, and into a format that they can actually use. There are undoubtedly further challenges staring at them right now. You can help them a little by becoming an individual member on their website. I've seen enough to be confident they'll survive.

What you might feel you need to know...

In the course of writing this book, showing it to other people and considering how it had all come together, it became increasingly obvious that people were going to ask questions about my background, and the perspective I'm coming from in writing it.

To be honest, I didn't set out to write something so loaded with politics. My primary interest is in niche football: in the passions that collide when teams that mean everything meet, something I've found over the years is often as good outside the big, widely-supported clubs as it is within them. Still, since I've ended up writing about areas that I know some will find contentious, I'm going to take a second to outline the key things about where I'm coming from. You'll have your own views on what this all means, but perhaps this will help you to understand mine.

I'm primarily a football fan drawn to CONIFA's very nature. For the last decade, a passion for sport and a passion for travel have often collided in my life. Back in 2003, I ran the Rome marathon the day after catching Lazio against Inter in Serie A, having grown up watching Channel 4's football Italia. My sporting travel adventures have since taken me to see a team I'm a little besotted with, St Pauli, play Union Berlin in Hamburg. I also watched a South Korea v North Korea world cup qualifying derby in Seoul, a game in which the South Koreans pulled together vocal faux 'away' supporters to make up for their political rivals' inability to travel. They drew 0-0 in that game, and also in Pyongyang, in qualifiers for the 2010 World Cup. The goalless stalemates were almost suspiciously tame, and both teams went on to qualify, first and second in the Asian qualifying group.

I've had season tickets at FC Seoul, having lived in South Korea for nearly two years, and several years' worth of them at Aston Villa, my childhood club. Having grown up in Salisbury, I also have a soft spot for Salisbury City, and more recently the phoenix club that occupy their ground now, Salisbury FC, managed by the ever-lively striking legend Steve Claridge.

I've lived in Dublin since 2008, though, with my lovely wife, who I met during my time in Seoul. The city sits conveniently between her home and mine: Salisbury, and the rural West of Ireland. I'd been writing for years before I started writing about sports, but one day in 2015 I persuaded the Dublin Gazette to take a chance on me, and I've been submitting sports stories across all flavours of sport their way ever since, usually at a rate of 3-4 a week.

That's opened my eyes to amateur sport. I'm crazily passionate about GAA, and almost invariably the only foreigner in the Croke Park press box. When it comes to football, I still drop home to see Aston Villa when I can, but most of the games I watch live are either in the League of Ireland, Ireland's semi-pro top two tiers, or (more often) the regional Leinster Senior League. My favourite game ever, in fact, involved a local Dublin side, Tolka Rovers, coming from 2-1 down in injury time in the last game of the season to avoid relegation to the Irish fourth tier. They won 3-2, the last goal coming from a halfway line lob. Their opponents, Glebe North, had won the return leg 8-0 earlier in the season, but nevertheless went down in Tolka's place.

My obscure football passion means like some of the CONIFA executive, I have a wardrobe full of football shirts most people wouldn't recognise, ranging from an El Salvador and Zanzibar national shirts picked up on my travels, to a Great Britain Olympics shirt and a once-off green Aston Villa away shirt produced by the Irish supporters' club.

It was that trip to St Pauli, though, that turned me on to CONIFA. The socialist, old-school club still had a little bit of merchandise around their insane Millerntor Stadium - situated, naturally, on Hamburg's red-light district - relating to the FIFI Wild Cup, a summer tournament played back in the summer of 2006, which saw teams like Gibraltar (now a UEFA member) take on current CONIFA members Greenland, Tibet and Northern Cyprus, and a team representing St Pauli themselves.

I was immediately hooked on the concept, and later discovered an odd quirk of fate: Sacha Duerkop, the General Secretary of CONIFA, also missed this tournament and learnt of it later, and is an avid St Pauli fan.

This book, though, does not come from a place of great knowledge about CONIFA built up over years, but is the product of an enthralled few months of intensive research and a lot of conversations with people who matter inside the organisation. About 35 hours of interviews, in total, as well as attendance in London. I am, now, a CONIFA member, but this is largely because they were kind enough to grant me endless interviews and a press pass that got me into seventeen games on the promise of this book. I thought the €25 membership fee was the very least I could give back.

I don't have strong views on the political ambitions that connect to most of these sides, though having spent a wonderful few days in Dharamshala, the seat of the exiled Tibetan government in India, I do have a real soft spot for the Tibetan cause.

I have never travelled to Russia or any of its separatist regions. I have never travelled to Northern Cyprus (though I have been to Turkey). I have travelled to North Korea, twice, though it was years ago, and the place fascinated me, but didn't particularly impress me. I have never travelled to Algeria, the part of Turkey with Armenian roots, or Matabeleland. In fact, scanning the full list of CONIFA's members, the only ones I can think of any associations or experience of other than Tibet and the Korean entry are Zanzibar (where I went for my honeymoon), Yorkshire (I'm English), Padania (in that I've taken a holiday in that corner of Italy) and Panjab (a backpacking trip in 2007 took in Amritsar).

Most of you, of course, won't care one bit about the above, and that's absolutely fine. I'm genuinely glad you can read about something like CONIFA in that way. If you talk regularly online about this tournament, though, you'll quickly learn that some people view any kind of backing of CONIFA as being a political act. The above is really aimed at these people.

For those who might have read the last few hundred pages trying to gauge my view (or, if you're feeling harsh, my 'political agenda'), I wasn't trying to hide it, so much as to be neutral towards an inherently heavy (at times) scenario. If you were wondering, I'm a bit of a lefty (which is probably clear from the love of St Pauli). I'm broadly in favour of self-determination, but I also recognise that in some cases that can be a gross simplification of a situation.

Above all, though, I really want to emphasise that I care about football, and I care about the huge passion behind some of these teams. I care about their ability to play football, because I see how much they care about it, and it's kind of impossible not to get sucked in. I've never seen anything quite like it. But like CONIFA, I'm here to observe the politics, but not to take part.

If you need to know more than that, you can ask me yourself.

I'm on Twitter at @jameshendicott, or you can email jameshendicott.jh@gmail.com.

Thanks for buying my book, I'm extremely proud of it, and I hope you enjoyed it.

James

The making of CONIFA: Football for the Forgotten

In order to research and write this book, I travelled to London from my home in Dublin for ten days in late May and early June 2018. I'm English, but that's the longest I've spent in the UK in nearly a decade.

Over the course of those ten days, I spent much of my time enjoying the hospitality of CONIFA and the volunteer staff, as well as Sutton United, Bromley, Carshalton Athletic, Enfield Town, Haringey Borough and Fisher football clubs, sometimes several on the same day. I am grateful for their welcome and help.

I did not travel to other host venues Slough Town, Bracknell Town and Aveley FC due to match clashes and travel constraints. In total, over nine days, I spent more than 24 hours on public transport, watched roughly 1500 minutes of live football, and witnessed upwards of 50 goals.

Due to the compact nature of the CONIFA World Football Cup, it is not possible to see substantially more than a third of games live, and so CONIFA's excellent video coverage (provided by FC Video) has also been extremely helpful in piecing together the action at games I didn't attend.

In the course of the tournament, I saw every one of the sixteen teams play, some just once, and others in as many as four of their six contests. All the teams were highly approachable, and a number took the time to explain to me in detail the origins of their squads, and their claim to nationhood.

I also received a great deal of assistance from others in the press box, and would particularly like to thanks Steve Clare and Ali Gilmore (from Prost Publishing, who spent the tournament following Cascadia, and were endless sources of knowledge on their side), JD Singh and Chris Walker (of KLFC radio, and excellent sources of knowledge on Panjab), who stepped away from their own responsibilities to help me out.

CONIFA themselves, in particular through President Per-Anders Blind, General Secretary Sascha Duerkop, press man Kieran Pender and Director Paul Watson, were exceptionally helpful.

Stephen Findlater, who took me on as a novice sports writer at the Dublin Gazette in 2015 - I had already been working in music and travel journalism for 8 years - spotted something in my love of amateur sport, and has been endless helpful in getting me where I am today.

My literary agent, Melanie Michael-Greer, came to me after I had announced and set about producing a self-published version of this book. She saw in me, and in the concept, far more than I had the confidence to see myself, and her help has taken the book to new heights.

My brother, Thomas and his fiancé Emily - two successful lawyers with little interest in football - tolerated ten days of late arrivals, CONIFA chat and inconvenience as I occupied their back room. Stephen Byrne, who helped out with editing, and David Dooley, who designed the cover, were both wonderful.

Most of all, I'd like to thank my wife Helena and young son Adam, who was four at the time of the tournament. They spent four days in London with me, and six alone back in Dublin while I hopped from stadium to stadium.

Helena supports my dreams, and Adam greets me like I was never gone, simply eager for a story and a play. Their tolerance of my chasing this dream has been astounding, and their support invaluable. I couldn't ask for anything more.

And Finally

This book could never have come to pass without the several dozen people of blind faith who bought it, unseen, in an act of faith ahead of and during my trip to London in 2018. A huge, huge thank you to all of the following, whose financial backing helped this see the light of day…

Ron Huiberts ↔ Nick Bec ↔ Justin McDaid ↔ Mary Geoghegan ↔ Christopher O'Keeffe ↔ Sean Smyth ↔ Sean Noone ↔ Robert McKenna ↔ Christopher Marsh ↔ John Corbett ↔ John Smith ↔ Craig McDonnell ↔ Adrian Steele ↔ Dickon Court ↔ Adam Flynn ↔ Chris Trevor ↔ Jasper Mispelters ↔ Dean McGarry ↔ Mary Fitzpatrick ↔ Fionnuala Jones ↔ Claire Hendicott ↔ Ben Hayes ↔ Karl Greenway ↔ Leonard Laymon ↔ Christopher Piper ↔ Kevin Morris ↔ Jonathon Chedgzoy ↔ Jess Cully ↔ Fairless Schofield ↔ Christopher Forsythe ↔ Vanessa Monaghan ↔ Oisin Tormey ↔ Declan Marron ↔ Aaron Johnsen ↔ Simon Gorman ↔ JD Singh ↔ Bryan O'Hanlon ↔ Colin Weston ↔ DP Bolt ↔ Ramush Ganohanti.

L - #0240 - 260421 - C0 - 210/148/12 - PB - DID3074466